Bill,

To a longtime friend and one of the <u>best</u> people I know.

Bill

Everything You've Heard About Investing Is Wrong!

Everything You've Heard About Investing Is Wrong!

How to Profit in the Coming Post-Bull Markets

WILLIAM H. GROSS

TIMES BUSINESS

RANDOM HOUSE

Library of Congress Cataloging-in-Publication Data
Gross, William H.
Everything you've heard about investing is wrong! :
how to profit in the coming post-bull markets
William H. Gross. — 1st ed.
p.   cm.
Includes index.
ISBN 0-8129-2839-3 (acid-free paper)
1. Investments.   2. Finance, Personal.   I. Title.
HG4521.G745   1997
332.6—dc21   96-50901

Random House website address: http://www.randomhouse.com/

Printed in the United States of America on acid-free paper

98765432

First Edition

Designed by Robert C. Olsson

To my wife, Sue, who has been with me since my dawning and has given me the happiest thirteen years of my life. If there be a heaven, I have caught a glimpse of it through you. You have my constant love and enduring respect.

To Jeff, Jenn, and Nick, my three wonderful children, two of whom are now fully grown and one who thinks he is. Keep looking for that golden egg, but make sure not to pass by the chocolate ones. They add up and are the foundation of a life well spent. I have high hopes and endless love for each of you.

To my mom, Shirley Karpen: having kids, I've learned, is a lot of work, and I was certainly a handful. Thanks for your devotion and love through all these years. You have mine as well.

Acknowledgments

An author needs many things, but above all he needs an audience, and I have been more than fortunate through these many years at PIMCO. I can't recall how many loyal readers of my *Investment Outlook* have said, "You should write a book, you know." My thanks to all of you—clients and associates alike—who have encouraged me for at least a decade.

An author also needs an able and enthusiastic assistant willing to put in long hours on the computer, revising graphs and correcting grammar as well as interfacing with insistent editors and the outside world. Danelle Reimer has done all of that and more for me and has left her footprints on this book along with many others too countless to name.

Contents

Contents

Introduction

We've been living in an age of high-octane financial markets. A bull market in stocks since the mid-1970s, combined with a dramatic performance for bonds since 1981 and the days of Paul Volcker, has convinced Americans that the way to get rich is to invest in "the market." Such times have come before, of course: the South Seas Bubble, the Roaring Twenties, and the real estate frenzy of 1975–1985 were all times when investors and speculators thought they couldn't lose—that all they had to do was belly up to the bar and slap their $2 down on the counter, and a beer and $4 change would come back before they had a chance to say "Intel."

I'm here to tell you that it's just not that easy. This "Era of Money" has been almost unique. For one thing, the twenty-year bull market in stocks and the fifteen-year run-up in bonds have been longer than almost any comparable period in world history. Sure, we had our 1987 stock market crash and the 1994 debacle in bonds, but they were short and corrective as opposed to drawn-out and stagnant. Second, the conditions that produced these long bull markets will be difficult to duplicate in the future. They were caused by a sharp increase in corporate profits combined with a near-historic drop in inflation and interest rates. Since the mid-1970s, after-tax profits have increased by 10 percent annually. And since 1981, inflation has receded from double digits to a lowly 2 to 3 percent a year, while long-term Treasury yields plunged from 15¼ percent in 1981 to 6 percent in 1993. This performance will not be repeated in our lifetimes.

There'll be a lot of disappointed investors out there if they expect a repeat of the past two decades. The Era of Money is about to come to a close. Not in a dramatic way, though. This is not a book about the coming Depression of 1998 or the Crash of '99. It's not meant to scare you or to get you to rush out and sell your stocks and bonds and replace them with greenbacks, diamonds, or gold. Instead, this book will describe the coming new era, an era already dawning, during which you'll likely compound your money at 6 percent rates as opposed to the 15 to 20 percent rates that have been synonymous with our rapidly maturing bull markets.

The Era of 6 Percent

Humorist Will Rogers once said, "I'm more concerned with the return *of* my money than the return *on* my money." He made that crack during the Great Depression, the longest and worst period of business stagnation in our history. The future is not going to be quite as bad as that. Your investments will still offer a handsome return relative to inflation—just not what you may be used to. The next era will be the "Era of 6 Percent." Still, getting that kind of return and keeping it, as Will Rogers might have encouraged, will not be easy. Purchasing high-flying stocks soon destined to fall, being too conservative by holding 4 percent CDs, and paying excessive fees for professional investment management are just three ways to ensure that you won't keep up with the Joneses in the battle for investment profits over the next decade. In order to excel, you'll need an understanding of the global economy in the coming years—an appreciation for what could produce *disinflation* as well as the accelerating inflation you're still probably afraid of and which type of environment favors stocks and which bonds. The old adage "Stocks always outperform bonds" is pure bunk, and you should know why bonds may be relatively good investments in the coming years. You'll also need to know which bonds to buy and how to reach for yield without sacrificing safety. Last, but certainly not least, you should know that *you* are an important part of the quest for 6 percent. Your psychological makeup, your patience or impatience, your need to "play the game," or your willingness to sit back and let your profits run are all part of the equation that will add up to mediocre or exceptional returns.

I hope this book will help you grab the long end of the stick. It reflects what I've learned in the past twenty-five years of investing for the clients of Pacific Investment Management Company. It's also a prediction of what lies ahead in the "forecastable" future—the next three to five years, into the start of the twenty-first century. Each chapter begins with a personal commentary about this or that—the meaning of life, how it feels to be "scalped alive," and a host of other topics. I've always felt that reading about investing should be fun, and my stories aim to entertain as well as instruct. I hope you like my book and learn something at the same time. It should be an enjoyable—and profitable—way to enter the Era of 6 Percent.

PART ONE

Good-bye to the Super Bull

ONE

Back to Butler Creek

Investing in the Coming Era of 6 Percent

I've never lived near a river. The closest I ever got, I suppose, was Butler Creek in the backwoods of Middletown, Ohio, when I was a boy. It was gentle and kind, and its surprises came in the form of crawdads and salamanders and all sorts of fun things that little boys dream pleasant dreams of. There were no nightmares on the banks of Butler Creek—no floods, no levees, no sandbags, no shattered lives, and no presidents offering condolences. It was not the Mississippi of 1993. My summers were filled with running *to,* not *from,* the water. There were fish to catch in the deep eddy underneath the exposed roots of what had to be the county's biggest, oldest oak tree. There were BB guns to shoot at my brother, many make-believe bad guys lurking in the underbrush, lots of turtles to find, an abandoned shack that quickly became a fort, and buckeyes to pick. I've never lived near a river.

Now I live by the ocean. Friends joke that the next tsunami will sweep my house away like the Mississippi rolling through Saint Louis, but I know better. It's fifty yards from the Pacific and as untouchable as the homes of all my neighbors sequestered behind the gates of Irvine Cove. My children surf, make sand castles, look for crabs, and do all the other fun things that kids dream pleasant dreams of. There are trees to climb, parks to play in, a bike to ride for my little guy, Nick, and nice cars to drive for Jeff and Jennifer, my twenty-somethings. They've never lived near a raging river.

Will they ever? I don't know. As a parent with fifty-two years of life experience, I sometimes think the ideal would be for them to experience a few mild floods before they're thirty-five or forty so that they'll know how nice a gentle creek is during the second half of their lives. That's hard to arrange, though. You don't intentionally throw your kids into a raging torrent. Kicking them out of the house at twenty-one is one thing, but when they're hurting and you can help, it's oh so hard to say no, even when you realize that in the long run, a "no" would be the better response. But even if you try, life can't be engineered so smoothly. It's full of hard knocks and heartaches, even for kids who live in Irvine Cove, and no matter how many sandbags you have, you sometimes just can't build the levee high enough.

Surfing the Mississippi

Investment managers have lived in their own privileged world for the past fifteen years or so, when all you really had to do was "own the market" in order to look good. Being a superstar investor might have been as easy as being fully invested, packing your suitcase, and enjoying an extended vacation on the French Riviera. Usually, life (and managing money) is just not that easy. When the flood comes or the tide changes, you'd better be prepared. It's important to be an investor for *all* seasons.

Not many of us are. Professional investors, just like kids, may need a few hard knocks to focus their attention and to prove to themselves and their public that it's not just a bull market that's responsible for their success. Those knocks typically come in the form of bear markets that test how adaptable investors really are. If a manager's portfolio doesn't change, if his philosophy is simply to stay 100 percent invested and let the market bail him out at some future date, it's difficult to believe he ever had much expertise to offer in the first place. An index fund, which merely tracks the market while charging much lower management fees, would be much more profitable for its clients in the long run. No, an investor for all seasons needs the ability to recognize changing circumstances—not necessarily to change his or her philosophy but to adapt that philosophy to changing times. If you're a bottoms-up stock picker, fine. But you need to adjust your stock holdings consistently with your view of economic conditions several years forward. If you're a corporate bond manager, fine. But make sure you know when corporates do well and when they don't, and modify your holdings accordingly.

Which brings me back to Butler Creek. The opening paragraphs of this chapter contrasted the stream near my old backwoods home with the mighty Mississippi of 1993, which ravaged much of the Midwest. One was calm and placid, the other a raging torrent. In a way, they represent two significantly different types of investment markets.

For fifteen years now, we've experienced the turbulence of one of the strongest, most dynamic bull markets stock investors have ever known. From its level of 800 in 1981, the Dow Jones Index of industrial stocks has multiplied over 8 times, and other major indices have done as well or better. There've been a few waterfalls along the way, of course—October 1987 the largest—but for the overwhelming preponderance of the time, stocks have done nothing but go up.

Since September 1981, bonds have followed a similar pattern. Bond investors will remember 1994's bear market for a while, but it was really only a temporary reaction to a long-term fundamental trend that saw the interest on long-term Treasuries peak at 15¼ percent in 1981 and go as low as 5¾ percent in late 1993. That long-term trend produced an 80 percent appreciation in long-term bond prices, while the '94 bear market took back just 25 percent of those gains. Despite that setback, total returns for long Treasuries have come close to matching that of the stock market over the same period.

If a market can be compared to a river, then the past two decades, in both bonds and stocks, have certainly resembled the

THE SAVVY INVESTOR:

Bonds Ride the Teeter-Totter

Investors who don't deal with bonds on a daily basis often find the relationship between interest rates and bond prices quite confusing. What does it mean when a TV commentator says the bond market was up? Did *interest rates* go up, or did *prices* go up, as they say for stocks? The confusion comes about because interest rates (that is, yields) and bond prices move in opposite directions—much like a child's teeter-totter.

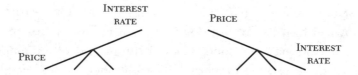

When yields go up, bond prices go down, and vice versa. The longer the maturity, the greater the move. To make it simple, picture short maturities as being near the teeter-totter's fulcrum. They don't move much, do they? Long bonds ride the ends of the see-saw. Their prices get quite a wild ride if interest rates on the other side go up or down.

Now that you know about the teeter-totter, you know the answer to my question. If the bond market is up for the day, what rises—prices or yields? Prices!

Mississippi of 1993—not in destructive force but in power, breadth, and certainly length. Both bull markets have been among the largest and most profitable in history. Because of that, most investors and money managers expect much the same in future years: double-digit returns and markets that are unidirectional on the upside. It's just not going to happen. What we're going to see instead are markets that more closely resemble my old backwoods haunt of Butler Creek: calm and placid, with little turmoil and, in financial market terms, relatively low total rates of return. To get specific, stocks should return 8 percent and bonds 6 percent over the next three to four years, compared to 15 percent–plus annualized total returns for both since the early 1980s.

T H E S A V V Y
I N V E S T O R :
Total Return

Total return is a concept that's difficult to comprehend for many investors. When they think about bonds, for instance, they tend to think of their return as simply a bond's "yield." That's primarily true only if the bond is held to maturity. Even then, if the periodic interest payments are reinvested at a different yield, the compounded return will vary.

A bond's true total return is composed of its interest payments plus its price appreciation or loss. If you measure total return annually, you need to add the bond's price change for the year to its interest rate yield to get a true calculation. When I speak of the Era of 6 Percent, I am referring to the *total* return for bonds, not simply to their yield.

For stocks, the calculation is much the same, except that dividend yield is substituted for interest: price change plus dividend yield equals total return. I believe that, in the near future, stock prices will probably go up by 6 percent a year and their average dividend yield will be 2 percent: 6 + 2 = 8 percent total return, just slightly better than that of bonds.

Very few money managers and investors active today have experienced the environment we are about to live through. They have navigated one river only, and they are ill prepared for the clear water we are about to experience. We are, in my opinion, headed downstream toward a shallow creek, not a torrential river. We've shot the rapids, gone over the waterfall of plunging interest rates and roaring stock prices, and are now about to navigate a far more calm and placid stream than any we've experienced since the late 1950s. We are going back to Butler Creek.

Why the Salad Days Are Over

It is not hard to understand why. As Einstein might have said, the mathematics are quite compelling. In the bond market, for instance, returns over long time periods are significantly influenced by the yields available when the starting gun goes off. If you begin with 15 percent yields, as we did in 1981, the likelihood of 15 percent total return over the next five to ten years is fairly high. There are no guarantees, of course, because bond market *total* returns depend on *fu-*

ture yields. They are influenced not only by the reinvestment of interest payments every six months forward but by the future price of the bond as well. Still, the starting point is highly influential. Those 15 percent yields in 1981 eventually led to almost 15 percent total returns ten years later, as seen in Figure 1-1. This graph displays average total bond returns for ten-year periods beginning in 1970. Lo and behold, by 1991, ten years after long-term Treasuries peaked at a yield of 15 percent–plus in 1981, the total return for the decade came close to the period's original yield.

FIGURE 1-1.
AVERAGE ANNUAL TOTAL RETURN
OF U.S. BONDS (TEN-YEAR PERIODS)

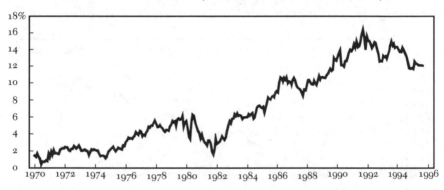

Source: Bridgewater Associates.

Today's Treasury yields of 5 and 6 percent, then, give you a pretty good idea what your return might look like as you jump ahead on the calendar, even over a shorter time frame such as between 1997 and the end of the twentieth century. A five-year Treasury note, to get specific, at a yield of 6 percent in 1996, should return close to 6 percent when it matures in 2001. The longer-maturity notes and bonds are a little more problematic, because in 2001 they'll still have quite a few years left before they come due, and the yield at that time will affect their current price. Even so, the changes in interest rates in the interim would have to be fairly dramatic to push the figure substantially above or below the starting yield.

A similar analysis of potential stock returns can be done by calculating the market's dividend yield in combination with estimated earnings growth. With a beginning dividend yield of close to 2 percent, one has only to estimate the future path of earnings to come up with a rough approximation of total returns. Of course that's not a simple task, but over the last seventy years, the growth rate in earnings for the Standard & Poor's 500 has been 6.1 percent, as shown in Figure 1-2. Adding the two produces a total return of just over 8 percent. With price/earnings (P/E) ratios slightly above historical norms, it takes only a minor downward adjustment to get to my 8 percent forecast for stocks through the end of the twentieth century.

FIGURE 1-2.
U.S. CORPORATE EARNINGS GROWTH

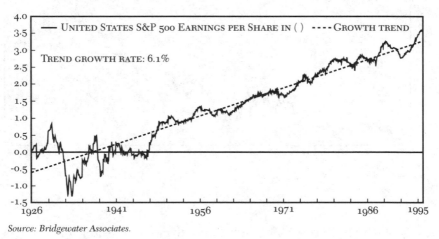

Source: Bridgewater Associates.

But the argument for Butler Creek does not rest on a mathematical foundation alone. More critical to my argument is the economic setting. In order to envision returns for bonds of around 6 percent and for stocks in the vicinity of 8 percent, what is really needed is a substantially different *economy* than the one that produced our roller-coaster markets over the past fifteen to twenty years. The economy of the 1970s was characterized by easy money and accelerating inflation, that of the 1980s by tight money and disinflation. The dramatic transition from one to the other shot yields up to 15¼ percent for long Treasuries in 1981 and then down to 5¾ percent in 1993. The fact is, over many three- or four-year stretches, a bond investor could have received negative total returns *or* as much as 18 percent annually, depending on whether inflation was moving higher or lower. Stocks displayed the same volatility and then some.

The markets of the future will be different because the economy has changed. In a series of chapters beginning in Part II of this book, I'll explain why nominal economic growth (real growth plus inflation) should average a placid 4 to 5 percent through the balance of the century and why inflation should move around a 2 percent guidepost. That is really the key to Butler Creek: 5 percent nominal GDP growth and 2 percent inflation. Sure, we'll have a mild recession and a decent cyclical recovery between now and the year 2000, but not much more, and there'll be no sustained upward pressure on inflation to cause investors to flee bonds—or stocks, for that matter. I'll offer what I hope will be a compelling analysis of the following long-term trends that promise to hold inflation down:

1   Current high levels of debt that inhibit consumption
2   Capital market "vigilantes" who enforce monetary and fiscal discipline
3   An evolving demographic influence that fosters saving and spells an end to the "shop-till-you-drop" attitudes of U.S. consumers
4   A global trading environment that promotes low wage growth

ECONOMICS 101
Real Versus Nominal GDP

Discussions about the growth rate of our gross domestic product (GDP) are often confusing. For starters, economists and publications used to refer to it as GNP, or gross national product, but for some esoteric reason a name change was made several years ago. GDP is the total annual production of goods and services in our economy, and, of course, it changes every year. Those changes result in what is known as a GDP growth rate.

The GDP growth rate, however, can be stated in two different ways. *Real GDP growth* refers to the increase in goods and services once price inflation is subtracted out. *Nominal GDP growth* includes inflation. Therefore, as long as we have some inflation, nominal GDP will always be larger than real GDP.

Remember to discriminate between the two terms as they're used throughout this book.

Never before have these four dominant long-term trends been in such distinct alignment, and never before has that formation so adamantly argued for mild economic growth with no inflationary pressures. Thus, there is little reason to expect much change in interest rate levels. Inflation is the primary factor in determining interest rates, and if that doesn't change much in the next three to five years, total returns from bonds (interest and price movement) and total returns from stocks (dividends and price movement) will be muted as well.

Perhaps the most important thing investors must recognize is that our recent fifteen-year bull market in bonds and stocks has been due to *declining* inflation—what economists label *disinflation*. Almost every five years since 1981, there has been a discernible downward shift in inflation. Most of it, as Figure 1-3 depicts, occurred early in the 1980s, but there was a drop between 1984 and 1989 and another decline between 1990 and the present.

FIGURE 1-3.
U.S. INFLATION, 1960–1995

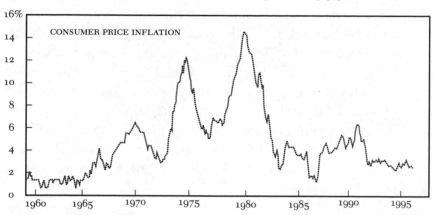

Source: The Bank Credit Analyst, *February 1996.*

This movement generated and perpetuated the bull market in bonds and stocks because *financial assets benefit more from the transition to lower inflation than from the actual lower inflation itself.* Because of the declining trend of inflation, bond prices accelerated, P/E ratios expanded, and corporate earnings moved up smartly. These are the ingredients, nay, the very definition, of bond and stock bull markets, but when two of the three disappear, the bloom comes off the bull market rose. When interest rates stop declining and bond prices no longer go up, P/E ratios cannot continue to move ever skyward; and when P/E ratios stabilize, stock returns are dependent on earnings growth, just as bond returns are dependent on their current yield. The result is a 6 to 8 percent world for bonds and stocks.

Sure—in one year you may get 15 percent return, and the next you'll get close to zero. On *average,* though, the returns are going to be nothing like you've been accustomed to. You've been spoiled! You've just lived through one of the greatest bull markets of all time, but the salad days are over. If you're expecting to earn 20 percent a year to pay for a second home or finance your kid's college education, forget it. Instead of going ballistic, you need to get realistic, and that's what this book's all about.

So come on in, the water's fine; it's just not that deep. It's a warm fall day, the corn's high in the fields, the livin' is still pretty easy. There are crawdads and salamanders in the creek, vines to swing on, even some fish to catch under the roots of the old oak tree. It's just not the Mississippi—that raging torrent you may have gotten used to over the past several decades. This is Butler Creek, the stream of 6 percent. In the next chapters, I'll take you on a guided tour of this gentle brook. I'll describe it in more detail, explain in simple economic terms why your investments are probably going to resemble a little brook in Middletown, Ohio, for the next five years, and give you a little insight as to how you should row your boat toward that uncertain future. Let's cast off.

TWO

Row, Row, Row Your Boat

Long-Term Thinking for the Smart Investor

"Remember just two things," an old friend once told me while I was struggling with a host of seemingly insurmountable problems. "One: Don't sweat the small stuff. Two: It's *all* small stuff." His advice produced an instant guffaw that soothed my short-term pain, but over the years it has become a source of serious personal reflection. There's a wallop packed into those two sentences that could keep philosophers or a slew of radio talk-show hosts busy for years. If it's all "small stuff" and life is but a dream, as the last line of the old song maintains, lots of gentle rowing is probably a great way to proceed down life's little brook. If, however, there's lots of small stuff and several *big* things, the pace quickens and a certain intensity is required. The trick, of course, is to determine what the big stuff might be and to recognize it when you see it—not necessarily an easy task for anyone who seriously ponders the meaning and ultimate outcome of existence.

I have concluded, as you may have guessed, that there's both a lot of small stuff in this world that shouldn't raise a sweat and a few very big things that demand focus and constant attention. What's intriguing and somewhat frustrating, however, is how relative and mercurial even those big things can be as you move down the stream. Breaking up with your teenage girlfriend was certainly very big stuff at seventeen, but it hardly causes a ripple in the memory bank a decade later as you settle into marriage and family building. Failing to get a promotion or that new job was a crushing blow in your thirties, but twenty years later is written off as perhaps having been for the best. A wife's or husband's extramarital affair may have nearly brought a marriage to the brink of divorce, but failing health and the need for companionship as one approaches 60 relegate the incident to the category of "just one of those things." Over time, a lot of big stuff becomes smaller stuff, and in a way my friend's classic two-liner makes sense. Maybe it *is* all small stuff!

But no, that can't be right. Life has no meaning if it's just a series of historical events that quickly lose their significance. What's wrong with the above analysis is that those events should never have been considered big stuff in the first place. The big stuff, aside from life's inevitable tragedies, is really the delicate, almost imperceptible fabric of feelings, thoughts, and actions that form the total of one's life. It has less to do with events—what things happen to people—than it does with behavior—how we react to them. It's not about individual successes and failures, but how you play the game. Do you deal with people fairly, with kindness, and with at least a modicum of selflessness, acknowledging a world outside your own existence? Do you come to peace with your maker and approach life's final harbor with hope for an infinite future? Or can you at least look back with some pride at how you rowed your boat down this earthly stream that flows to a most uncertain shore? That's the big stuff. The rest, in retrospect, is really not worth your sweat.

Investing with a Long-Term View

Few principles are more important in the world of investing than keeping your eye on the big stuff. Those who get bogged down in minutiae almost invariably lose, but investors who focus on the long-term picture improve their chances immeasurably, even in comparison to the pros. I learned this lesson early, even before I began to manage money in 1971. The year was 1966. I had just graduated from Duke University and had four months before I was due to show up at Navy boot camp. So I decided to go to Las Vegas and give professional blackjack a try. I'd studied the art of card counting my entire senior year in college. There had been little class time but lots of blackjack. And because I knew that the system I had mastered shifted the odds to me instead of the casinos, I felt I could approach blackjack as a profession as opposed to the more frivolous activity we call gambling.

Well, the blackjack and the winning all came together as planned, but I found that there were stretches of time—several hours, even a day or two—when I wouldn't win, and I'd become extremely discouraged. I'd sit around for hours wondering what was wrong, afraid to go back to the tables. I finally realized that when you have the odds in your favor, you need to take a long-term view. A short period of bad luck will almost always be offset by long favorable stretches. Instead of sitting out, I should have been playing all the time, letting the long-term outlook make money for me.

But when you talk about long-term horizons, it's important to define your time frame. Obviously, long-term investing has nothing to do with the images we all see on the TV business channels of traders with a phone to each ear, supposedly making lots of money. (I tried that technique once and found I couldn't understand what either ear was trying to tell me!) On the other hand, as Keynes once said, in the long term, we're all dead.

To me, that suggests that an investment horizon has to be longer than a few seconds but shorter than forever! I heard an ex–stock mutual fund manager forecast on TV the other day that the Dow Jones Industrial Average would reach 116,000! (As I write, the index is a bit over 6400.) When asked when, he just shrugged. "Some day," he implied. "All you have to do is wait!" I vehemently disagree with the many equity managers who claim that the best approach is always to stay fully invested because, over the long term, stocks will always go up. They feel it's impossible to time the market, so it's best to ride out the rough waves for the inevitable following wind. I'll agree with them on one thing: it's extremely difficult to "time" the market over the short term—and I rarely try. The biggest problem is mastering human emotion, primarily your own. At the bottom of a bear market, it's extremely difficult to overcome your fear and jump in with both feet—even assuming you have a reasonably good idea that you are at the end of the bear market! It's the same thing at the top: it's really hard to put a lid on Mr. Greed, even if you sense that things might just be getting too good.

There are times, though, when changes in an investment portfolio should be made—and that doesn't just mean selling the hot growth stocks and buying conservative large caps. You should be altering your bond/stock mix as well as raising or investing cash by focusing on a longer-term outlook. How long? Longer than a month, yes; longer than a year, sure; but something less than forever. The best way is to structure a portfolio within a long-term horizon of three to five years by looking at what I call *secular* factors. Now, I'm not going to talk religion here. I made a new business presentation several years ago to a group that, upon hearing my advocacy of a secular outlook, immediately questioned what God had to do with interest rates. I replied delicately, "I'm not really sure," but I went on to explain that "secular" in this case meant longer-term: at least three years, maybe as long as five. Anything longer than that, and you'd jump into the guesswork world of John Naisibitt and the futurists. Much shorter than that, and you'd have cauliflower ears—right and left—like those TV bond traders.

It's over this three-to-five-year time period that I think you can most appropriately structure a portfolio. Looking ahead several years sends your psyche the signal that investing is not a game but a serious long-term proposition. It also helps to reduce the fear and greed that affect many of our investment decisions. One of my investment heroes is a man named Jesse Livermore. I've got a picture of him behind my desk at work, top hat and all. He operated in the 1920s and early '30s, became a millionaire eight separate times, and went bankrupt just as many. He blew his brains out in a Wall Street bathroom in 1932, so you could call him the Ernest Hemingway of investing, I suppose. He was a strange sort of person to be anyone's hero. But he had a lot of brilliant things to say about investing in a classic book

THE SAVVY INVESTOR:

Secular Versus Short-Term Trends

Investing is a long-distance race, and because it is, investors should pattern their behavior after a marathon runner's—not a sprinter's. Marathoners pace themselves, plan ahead, and run within their physical limits. Investors must do the same. Because their goal is longer term, it seems only logical that the information they use to make decisions should have a *secular* range. "Secular" refers to trends that require years for their germination and culmination.

I like to think in terms of three-to-five-year time spans, because that is all investors can reasonably expect to forecast. For example, instead of focusing on one-month short-term trends such as housing starts, investors should analyze the secular trends in demographics that ultimately drive the long-term demand for new homes. Other secular trends include fiscal and monetary policy, trade balances, the strength or weakness of a nation's currency, and the evolving political leanings of its citizens.

called *Reminiscences of a Stock Operator.* One of his best insights was the following: "Throughout all my years of investing I've found that the big money was never made in the buying or the selling. The big money was always made in the waiting."

Forget about trading. Set your sights on a horizon and sail until you get there. My ideal horizon is three to five years because it eliminates the daily flow of emotion and allows you to focus on the important macroeconomic trends that are the primary movers of markets.

Important Secular Trends

What are some of these trends? The rest of this book will elaborate on many of them. One of my favorite areas of study is demographics—the slow, almost imperceptible movement of population trends: how many children are born and when, or the changing age at which most people buy their first house. These dull, seemingly arcane facts have nothing to do with today's business headlines about the latest power of a computer chip or the hot new movie from the Disney studio, but they're as powerful factors as you can find in determining the future of interest rates and stock prices.

Another secular trend has been the globalization of trade and finance. The world's ability to move production to cheap-labor ports of call has been instrumental in reducing inflation in the 1990s. For that, an analysis of the North American Free Trade Agreement (NAFTA) and the European Union suggests where free trade may be headed over the rest of the century.

Yet another secular consideration would be the growing influence of bond traders, or the "capital market vigilantes" as I like to call them. Their power over the past few years has changed the values of stocks and bonds enormously. Even Bill Clinton's 1992 campaign manager, James Carville, said that in his next life he wanted to come back as a bond trader (actually, he said he wanted to come back as the "bond market," but the entire market's a little too amorphous for even a Carville reincarnation).

Other secular factors include monetary policy, fiscal trends (How big will the deficit be?) and the potential strength and weakness of the dollar against other major currencies. If all this suggests you might need a refresher course in economics, you may be right. I've always said that a good institutional bond manager has to be one-third mathematician, one-third horse trader, and one-third economist. As an individual investor, you don't need to be all those things, but an appreciation of broad, secular economic factors helps enormously.

To put secular advice into perspective, take a look at Figure 2-1.

FIGURE 2-1.
WHOLESALE PRICE INDEX, 1779–1951

ALL COMMODITIES

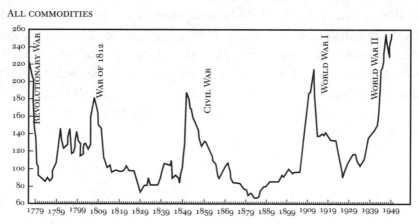

Source: *U.S. Historical Statistics, Bureau of the Census, Washington, D.C. 1975.*

It's an almost two-hundred-year history of commodity prices. The first thing that strikes me when I look at it is that this is a really *long* time. It's not your day-to-day update of the CRB commodity price index, which tells you whether or not it's been raining in the Midwest. It encompasses periods of recession and recovery, dramatic booms and depressions, inflation and deflation. Look at the dramatic run-up in prices during World War II. Something must have changed then. Was it Franklin D. Roosevelt and the beginning of the New Deal social and economic programs, a Federal Reserve that refused to allow significant recessions, or just the outbreak of war? Whatever your view, by looking at such a long-term chart, you begin to think about the long-term secular factors that influence markets. That is where the money is made: "in the waiting," as Jesse Livermore said.

But wait no longer when it comes to educating yourself on the secular outlook. Subscribe to some secular-thinking periodicals, such as *The Economist,* the respected, highly literate, and very readable British magazine of business and politics. Read some history books with a focus on economic history—there are quite a few good ones. (Some of my favorites are listed in the bibliography.) And subscribe to a service or two such as those provided by Ray Dalio at Bridgewater Associates and Ed Hyman at ISI, which offer up long-term charts and commentary on a host of economic statistics. You'll need more than this book to become successful in the investment arena. Whatever your reading habits and inclinations, get those phones away from your ears and start to focus on the next three to five years. It's not that far away, and you could be making some money by then. You need to stop sweating the small stuff and focus on a few big things. Row your boat in the direction of the long-term secular outlook.

PART TWO

The Economic Setting

THREE

The Eyes Have It

Economic Cycles Good and Bad

"It is easier for a camel to fit through the eye of a needle than it is for a rich man to pass through the gates of heaven."

The other day I had a conversation with a spirit about my taxes. Oh, I don't mean to suggest I have otherworldly powers or that my taxes were so high that I needed to consult with the H&R Block of the supernatural. But it was April 9, and I was signing off on one of the most horrendous tax returns in the history of humankind. (Not "mankind": my wife, Sue, was joint on this and bears equal responsibility.) "My God," I said to myself, and out of the clear blue appeared an apparition, a spirit dressed in an Uncle Sam–type costume.

What had caused me to utter the name of the Lord while signing my 1040 was the realization that I was paying almost half of my income mainly for the benefit of other people. Sure, some of it was going for "defense" and some was going to pay the salary of the villainous tax collector himself, but most of it was going to be transferred from my account to someone else's account in the form of Social Security, Medicare, government pensions, welfare payments, food stamps, and the like. "Okay, okay, I accept all of that," I immediately said, a 1990s conservative having finally been worn down by the "logic" of liberals. "But if I'm gonna pay it, at least I should get *credit* for it," thought I, and it was at that moment that the ghostly Uncle Sam appeared, who at first I thought was God but must now admit was probably a dim reflection of my conscience, feeble as it may be.

"Listen, God or Sam or whoever you are," I said, "didn't I just contribute half of my income to the poor, and shouldn't that garner me some points on the heavenly scorecard?"

"Perhaps," he said, "but it doesn't really count because it wasn't *voluntary*. When God spoke about the camel and the eye of the needle," he continued, "he didn't say anything about the tax collector. He was referring to the spirit of giving and the spirit of sacrifice."

"Well, now I'm confused," I thought. "You mean, Sam, that if I'd lived in the era of John D. Rockefeller—an era without income taxes—and had decided to voluntarily give away half of my income to the poor, I'd have a better chance of getting to heaven than I do now? I'd still have just as much money, but my 'spirit' count would be higher, is that it? And remember, Sam, it's not as though I *have* to work. Every day I punch that time clock, I punch it *voluntarily*, with half of my check going to the poor."

Sam's ghostly form seemed to grow weaker, more out of disgust than from having been worn down by the strength of my intellectual arguments. I decided to come clean for fear I'd lose this April apparition forever and perhaps be stuck with a Deloitte & Touche accountant instead. "All right!" I half screamed, "I really work for *my* half, and the other half is just a sort of slush—but it's a productive slush, a fertilizer of sorts, is it not? When will you ever be satisfied?"

"Give it *all* away," he said curtly, like some sort of heavenly Monty Hall with a fist full of the sponsor's cash instead of his own. But then I knew I had him, that his camel and his needle belonged back in biblical days and not in the twentieth century. "If I gave it all away," I fired back, "what would remain of private investment, of capital, and the ability to provide jobs? What would be left for seed corn instead of corn on the cob?"

It was getting late in the day, and we had nearly exhausted each other in this spiritual debate. "I never met the Man myself," said Sam, "so I don't really know whether He's changed his mind about taxes and giving in this age of capitalism. Why don't we say this: pay your taxes, give more than you think you should, and pray that God's a twentieth-century economist. If He's still riding camels, then you, sir, had better start looking for a needle with a mighty big eye."

A Debtor's Prison

While I search for the needle with the world's most humongous eye, let's talk about a topic that can be just as taxing: debt. More than 10 percent of our taxes these days goes to support the national debt in the form of interest expense in the federal budget. And as Uncle Sam and we all know, going into debt can be an intoxicating experience. In the initial stages, those first few IOUs, like the first few drinks, make you giddy with pleasure. All the things those credit cards can buy! When the bills start coming due, however, a mild depression sets in. After you sleep it off and realize that you need a second job just to stay even, the effects can be downright sobering.

ECONOMICS 101
Total Debt

There are a lot of borrowers out there. The headlines usually imply that our federal government is the biggest debtor of them all, and that is true if you think of Uncle Sam as a single entity. But there are lots of other borrowers, including state and local governments, which issue municipal bonds; corporations, which borrow in the bond market and from banks; and individuals, who run up credit card debt and take out mortgages on their homes.

When you add the amounts owed by all these debtors, you come up with what is known as total U.S. debt. Debt, of course, does *not* include equity, corporate net worth, or the value of stocks on the open market.

We Americans take no backseat to any other nationality when it comes to the number of potential members of DA—Debtors Anonymous. We're up to our eyeballs in debt, not only individually but collectively. Not only is consumer debt at record levels, but federal and state government debt has reached new peaks as well. And while corporations are beginning to reduce their spending and borrowing, many still have tires around their waistlines that signal too much eating and not enough sit-ups. You can see the sorry history of total debt accumulation over time in Figure 3-1.

The United States is not the only offender, of course. The world in general has been on a borrowing binge for decades, as seen in the debt of members of the Organization for Economic Cooperation and Development (OECD) since 1970 (see Figure 3-2). In Europe, the successive step-by-step extension of the welfare state went on through the 1970s and '80s even as it became obvious that free lunches were in fact very costly. It's only now, with the surging power of the capital market vigilantes (see Chapter 4), that the ability of governments to continue offering a freebie banquet has been held in check, if not reversed.

Japan's debt has also accelerated over the years, but for different reasons. Its debt bubble has been a distinctly internal one generated by corporations and individuals placing leveraged bets on real estate

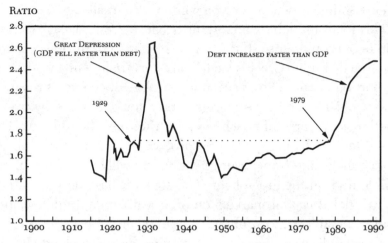

FIGURE 3-1.
TOTAL DEBT DIVIDED BY GDP, 1900–1990

Source: Bridgewater Associates.

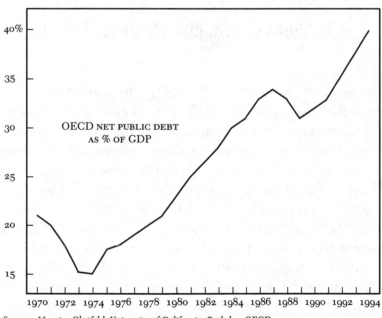

FIGURE 3-2.
LIVING ON BORROWED TIME

Sources: Maurice Obstfeld, University of California, Berkeley; OECD.

and the stock market. Whatever the reason, though, industrialized nations have been on a binge and their waistlines are overflowing. Richard Simmons, where are you when you're really needed?

This focus on debt is important because economies grow faster when debt is on the rise. If debt growth is limited, the chances for a slow-growth Butler Creek scenario are materially enhanced. A sizable portion of our nation's accounts payable, of course, is related to demographics, such as the mortgage creation generated by twenty-somethings in search of new houses for their new households. That, as we'll see in Chapter 5, is in the process of heading downhill. Another chunk comes from government, which will borrow any amount possible if given the green light. The signal is flashing yellow, however, as global capital markets enforce a discipline unfelt in prior decades. In addition, consumers in general are in no position to assume new obligations because their wages have stagnated and they simply cannot afford an increase in monthly payments. For all of these reasons, debt growth should slow and with it the growth of our national and world economies.

Virtuous Circles and Vicious Cycles

To visualize how this happens, it's helpful to understand what are known as the *virtuous circle* and the *vicious cycle*. The virtuous circle is the economic equivalent of a perpetual Good Samaritan: one good turn leads to another and another; and because we're talking about a circle here, I suppose "what goes around, comes around" would not be far off the mark as a description, either. Basically, this circle begins with some type of positive thrust or even shock to the economy. Let's say it's the mid-1970s, for instance, and the baby boomers, who are moving into their late twenties, are getting ready to buy that first home. Housing starts increase and with them the need for lumber, cement, and insulation, as well as the labor that produces them. Wages increase, profits go up, and the virtuous circle is under way. The higher wages allow construction workers to buy new cars, which leads to greater production in Detroit and more hiring at Ford and GM (and Toyota) as well. At the same time, accelerating corporate profits lead to additional investment in plant and equipment, which produces overtime at machine tool companies in Cincinnati. And so it goes, on and on, one positive step leading to another and another: a virtuous circle of growth (see Figure 3-3).

FIGURE 3-3.
A VIRTUOUS CIRCLE OF GROWTH

As these increases in hiring and investment take place, consumers and businesses, as well as government, become more aggressive in their willingness to borrow money. A full-time job with the prospect of good annual raises can make a family decide to stretch their payments in an attempt to capture the American dream. CEOs of corporations are willing to take on more debt because their company's stock price is high and rising and management is brimming with confidence. Government can borrow more because the voters hardly bat an eye at increasing public debt in the face of growing prosperity for all. This virtuous circle almost by definition leads to an expanding economy propelled even faster by an acceleration of debt and borrowing by individuals, businesses, and government. Ultimately, it can and usually does lead to near-full employment, high capacity utilization—and rising inflation.

But because of its effect on inflation, a virtuous circle is no Good Samaritan when it comes to the bond market. Bond investors are the vampires of the investment world. They love decay, recession—anything that leads to low inflation and the protection of the real value of their loans. A strong economy, however, spiked by an increase in debt, is like the sunrise—back into their coffins go the bond market vigilantes until night descends once more. As inflation soars, loans are repaid with dollars that are worth less, and the value of bonds declines.

The bond market ghouls are waiting for what is known as the vicious cycle—a mirror image of the positive circle I've just described. The difference is like, well—day and night. As with the virtuous circle, the beginning is often a demographic or policy shock that sets economic wheels in motion, but in the opposite direction. It can also begin simply because the positive circle has reached a point of excess. If debt levels, for instance, rise so high that lenders become reluctant to extend additional credit, the cycle begins to peak and ultimately reverse. Homeowners who have taken out second and third mortgages to keep the good life going now find the debt window closed because their home equity has eroded and lenders won't lend. Federal and state governments, constrained by too much debt and the increasing oversight of both voters and the bond market vigilantes, are forced to balance their budgets or at least move in that direction. Whatever the reason, be it demographic or a policy reversal, spending begins to fall, the pace of debt accumulation slows, and the vicious cycle begins. Capital spending drops, layoffs begin, and the economy's strength gradually or even suddenly declines. A bond vampire's dream is under way, because with lower growth come declining inflation and higher bond prices.

The Cycle of the Future

Let's return now to my opening illustration about the intoxication of debt and its ultimate hangover effects on economic growth. Are we in the giddy stage, somewhere within a virtuous circle, or are we about ready to reach for some aspirin as we enter a vicious cycle?

That's never easy to know, especially when viewing trends from a long-term *secular* outlook as opposed to a shorter-term business *cycle* perspective. Short-term growth or a recessionary economic cycle tends to mask secular acceleration or deterioration when the business cycle is moving in the opposite direction from the longer trend. It takes a careful eye and a focus on the longer term to filter out this superficial "noise." But the signs are now becoming fairly clear: debt at record levels seen previously only during the Great Depression; years of corporate layoffs driven by limited consumer spending power and the need to compete worldwide; negative demographics that encourage thrift and saving as opposed to more buying; twenty-somethings declining as a percentage of the population and buying fewer homes than did prior generations; and corporations reducing their debt in order to improve their balance sheets. All these signs point to a vicious cycle, though probably a mild one because of modern monetary policy and central banks' ability to reliquefy an economy. Take a look at Figure 3-4.

FIGURE 3-4.
NONFINANCIAL DEBT, 1955–1995

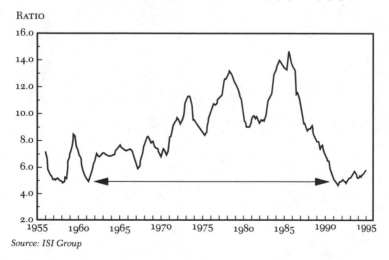

Source: ISI Group

This is a snapshot of total debt like the one at the beginning of the chapter, but this time expressed as a growth percentage and not as a percentage of GDP. It's also a much shorter historical perspective. It is apparent, though, that a change is under way and that debt is no longer growing as it did in prior periods. Note that a debt growth rate of 6 percent is the highest level the U.S. economy has been able to generate throughout this entire recovery (since 1990), whereas in prior recovery periods debt growth of 10 and 15 percent was the norm. The reason has been clearly explained: too much debt to begin with and the initiation of a mild vicious cycle sometime in the past five to ten years.

What does this mean for you as an investor? It means the Butler Creek scenario is alive and well. It means low rates of inflation throughout the balance of the century, a slow-growth economy, and attractive opportunities for bonds. And it means that the days of wine and roses for stocks are soon to end. Too much debt spells good-bye to double-digit returns on equities and a trip back for both bonds and stocks to that placid creek of the 1950s, when investors were satisfied with 6 percent, instead of 20 percent, returns.

FOUR

Easter Parade

Market Vigilantes and the Hunt for Investment Profits

Well, this year's "Grabfest"—more commonly known as our town's annual Easter egg hunt—is over, and I have sad, but predictable, news to report: we did *not* find the golden egg. I say "we," of course, with full accountability and more than a little shame. The fact is that I've been looking for that gilded symbol of superiority ever since I was a kid, and if I couldn't find it, well, then, my *kids* were going to find it. There's all sorts of vicarious pleasure out there to be had; the secret is in knowing where to look for it. Easter eggs might be at the bottom of most people's personal barrel, but what the heck, I'll give 'em a try, especially if there's a gold one to be had.

My experience with our older kids, Jeff and Jennifer, fifteen years ago taught me that what you have to do is show up at the park or golf course just a little bit early on Easter morning and casually walk around the egg-infested territory, pretending to enjoy the morning, the birds, or the advent of spring. You might hold your wife's hand or pose for a few pictures, but all the while your main focus should be on where the golden egg could possibly have been hidden *this* year. Last year, that snotty little girl with those overbearing parents found it at the foot of the giant oak between some obviously out-of-place

35

rocks. They won't hide it there again. And forget about any place too close to the starting line. They wouldn't risk having the thundering herd of five- and six-year-olds squash the egg just as the kiddie safari is under way. No, it's probably just past the tall grass, underneath some flowers that will be trampled after the rugrats have exhausted all the other possibilities. My youngest son Nick and I might as well stomp them into oblivion before someone else does.

Okay. The first step is to get him up to the front of the line. As they say in real estate—location, location, location. And when it comes to tracking down that prize of golden albumen, the same thing goes: if you're at the back of the line, you're nowhere. Bang! The gun finally goes off, and here we go, Nick. Don't worry about those chocolate eggs or the big jelly beans. I'll buy you some later. We're looking for a big *golden* egg that you can turn in to the Easter Bunny for a big surprise. Oh, God, look at all these other parents. Why don't they get out of the way and let their kids do the hunting? And there's that obnoxious Bob Johnson, looking under *our* flowers like he's into nature or something. Get outta there, pal—we were here first. And by the way, you're trampling the plants.

Someone found the silver egg? Ah, geez, this place gets worse every year. There's twice as many kids as there were last Easter. Nick, we've got to hustle now—get your hands off that chocolate egg, do you want to mess your clothes? Oh, hi there, Bob! Happy Easter to you, too. Your little guy sure looks cute. Someone found it? Under the bridge? Not that snotty little girl again—her parents must know the supervisor. I *cannot* believe it! What an example they're setting for their kids! Let's find Mommy and get out of here. And stop that whining. Do you want the Johnsons to see what a baby you are? I need to teach you about being a good sport.

Hi Ho, Silver!

There are all sorts of golden eggs in the real world, too, and many of them have been found in the financial markets over the past fifteen years. Owning an average bond or stock was like finding the silver egg, while latching onto a Microsoft or Intel was definitely golden. There are hundreds of thousands of hunters out there these days searching for the prize eggs; so many, in fact, that they've taken on a label: they're called the "vigilantes." I like to call them the "capital market vigilantes," which includes all those who like to hunt for bond, equity, and currency eggs. They are primarily institutional and mutual fund money managers who've come to power in the 1990s because of the tremendous amount of funds at their disposal, but also because of the breakdown of the concept of the nation-state and their lack of allegiance to any one country.

Collectively, they move billions upon billions of dollars from one investment and one country to the next, seeking the highest returns with the least risk, without any national allegiance. Their decisions create a lot of volatility in the markets but also enforce significant discipline over governments and central banks, forcing them to toe the line and clean up their fiscal acts. Their vigilance in dictating what they view as sound economic and legislative policies is essential to the Butler Creek outlook for stocks and bonds. Without them, there would be the risk of a return to inflation in future years, which would erode stock and bond prices quicker than you can say "Easter Bunny."

It was not always so, however. The birth of the vigilantes is due to the creation of a globalized trading environment and the concomitant breakdown of the nation-state. In the 1960s, 1970s, and even 1980s, it was much more difficult to move money back and forth across oceans and continents. Not only were mutual funds in their infancy but technology permitting the quick transfer of large sums of money was not in place. In addition, tariffs, taxes, and fees of all kinds were inhibiting forces. Perhaps most important, though, there was the concept of "country," as in "My country, 'tis of thee." Investors back then didn't seriously consider offshore investments, just as most Americans didn't consider buying a Toyota instead of a Ford. It was a question of allegiance and pride. You bought American because we were number one and you were helping to generate American jobs—maybe even your own job. Gradually, however, the mind-set began to change. Californians bought some Toyotas

and found them to be economical, high-quality cars. The word
spread, and gradually American citizens and investors began to take

ECONOMICS 101
The Global Capital Market

There have been global capital markets for as long as
caravans and ships have been able to move freely between one destination and another. In centuries past,
gold provided the basis of a rudimentary capital market system known as mercantilism, but today investors
strive to accumulate not only gold but assets such as
stocks, bonds, and real estate in almost any country in
the world.

While today's global investing at first blush appears
to be a simple process involving a phone call to your
hometown broker, it really is made possible by an intricate web of agreements among countries that allows
for the transfer of asset ownership across borders. In
some cases, taxes on dividends and interest earned by
foreigners are assessed by the home country, and
sometimes once your money moves into a country, you
can't take it out for a certain period of time. But by and
large, due to increasingly liberal laws and the advent of
computer technology, capital today moves around the
world at the speed of light, much like the TV program
that comes to you via satellite.

a closer look at many foreign products and even foreign stocks and bonds.

One way the transition can be seen is by harkening back to the presidency of John F. Kennedy. JFK was no friend of mine, but there's no denying his dynamism and ability to turn a phrase. "Ask not . . ." was one of the most inspiring oratorical two-liners ever. It defined not only his presidency but the balance of the decade, until the rebellion over the war in Vietnam and the advent of the love generation turned the focus toward less patriotic, more hedonistic pursuits. No baby boomer will ever forget that Boston-accented voice or that phrase on that January morning in 1961, and to question its validity requires a special brand of heresy, even in the 1990s, when "what you can do for your country" doesn't really speak to the draft or even the Peace Corps, but to more sociologically relevant issues such as AIDS, the homeless, and the environment. Kennedy's challenge, much like his eternal flame, lives on but with a different focus.

Yet there has been a change that perhaps even JFK would be forced to acknowledge were he alive today, and let me put it to you bluntly: What's my *country* got to do with it? In this age of global communications, homogeneous worldwide production, and mass (frequently illegal) immigration across borders, it's becoming increasingly unclear to whom or what we belong, to whom or what we owe allegiance. I'm an American, yes, but I happen to be an American who lives within a vast undefined territory of southwestern North America that might be labeled "Calexico." Many of my radio and television stations are in Spanish; some are in Japanese. At least 25 percent of the products I buy are imported, and so, I'll wager, are yours. I'm as concerned about Bosnia as I am about downtown Los Angeles, and in the final analysis I have to ask myself—and, of course, you in turn—what's wrong with that? Why should we ask only what we can do for our *country*? Why should we have to buy American or put America first, when America is in such a state of flux that we're not even sure what it is anymore? Who are *we*? It's becoming increasingly clear with every passing year that we are not so much Americans but a conglomerate of Balkanized communities. We're not a melting pot anymore but a tossed salad.

The Decline of the Nation-State

One could argue that the very concept of the nation-state as we've come to know it over the past several centuries is rapidly disintegrating. There was a time, of course, when there were no nations as we understand them today. In the waning centuries of the Middle Ages, there was the Holy Roman Empire, to which most of Europe and parts of Eurasia owed allegiance, but in the eyes of many no sovereign of any "nation" was legitimate until he had been confirmed by the Pope. The Reformation of Luther and Calvin and Gutenberg's printing press helped change all that. "I am publishing a book in the German tongue," Gutenberg proclaimed, casting aside Latin, Europe's unifying language, and elevating his country above the Church and the Dark Ages' amorphous empire. What we now know as Germany and dozens of other individual states were to be born over the next several centuries.

Now the process is moving in reverse, driven in part by new economic realities. Today, the globalized market stretches beyond the political authority of any one nation, and even governments are unsure about whose interests to promote. The United States is eager to have Honda and Mercedes locate plants in Tennessee and Alabama in order to foster job growth, while at the same time defending Chrysler and Ford in their attempts to crack the Japanese market. Economic life is becoming increasingly internationalized, and as a result the relationship between the state and its citizens is breaking down. If our government likes Honda, why can't we? In the final analysis, why can't world citizens prefer another government's economic policies or another region's culture or religion and vote that way with their investments as well as their feet? Now that times are tougher and globalization is creating increased opportunities to emigrate, the tempo of internationalization is picking up. In time of war, they used to call the abandonment of national loyalty treason; in peacetime they called it unpatriotic; but in the twenty-first century, we may define a new era by it, as the nation-state takes a backseat to globalization and mass immigration on a scale rarely experienced in world history.

Vigilantes in Control

This transition from nation-states to a global economy has, within the last decade, been accompanied by an agglomeration of financial assets never before experienced. When you combine that with computer technology that moves money electronically faster than you can say "sell," you have a generation of international mutual fund and hedge fund managers and stock, bond, and currency traders that has become known collectively as the vigilantes.

The term tends to give the impression of a posse or perhaps a rogue band of money managers picking out a target here or there and swooping in for the arrest—or perhaps the kill. That, of course, is not the case. While there may be a "group-think" mentality of vigilante investment behavior, there is certainly no coordinated decision making among the denizens of the new world market. I know few of my bond market contemporaries, and I have little idea what they think about the markets at any point in time. If they are perceived to be acting in unison, it is certainly a misperception. There is *never* unanimity in financial markets. That's what allows for a simultaneous buy and sell order execution—having one person eager to buy what another is eager to sell. But when there is buying or selling *pressure* in one direction or another, it comes as a result of Adam Smith's "invisible hand"—thousands of independent money managers reacting to economic statistics in independent, but at times fairly homogeneous, ways.

As a rule, the vigilantes are looking for a combination of high return and low risk. That, of course, is a money manager's dream that is almost never achieved, but you want to have as high a return and as little risk as possible. That combination is generally best achieved by investing in countries with the following characteristics: (1) economic policies that promote high real GDP growth; (2) a stable political environment; (3) a sound and disciplined central bank; (4) a competitive currency without potential sinkholes; (5) low amounts of debt; and (6) a legal system emphasizing protection of individual property rights. Finding all these conditions in one single country is extremely difficult. The only one today that comes close is, believe it or not, the United States! But, as I'll argue, though the risks in the United States may be low, the returns of 6 to 8 percent are not historically, nor even relatively, high, and thus other foreign markets with slightly more risk and higher potential returns should attract the funds of the world investment community as well.

The vigilantes, then, are going to move money back and forth between the United States and Germany, or Germany and Japan, or Japan and Thailand, in order to find what they perceive as the best current combination of risk and return. In so doing, they enforce a discipline on governments and their central banks that has recently become quite significant and often fairly onerous. Mexico in late 1994 was perhaps the most visible example. When that country's trade deficit ballooned and it became obvious that the peso was significantly overvalued, billions of dollars in international investments were pulled out within a matter of days, bringing the country to its knees. Not only did the country have to devalue its currency by 50 percent, it also had to agree to stringent terms regarding money supply growth and future deficits, producing a near depression for its citizens. If you think it was Bob Rubin and the U.S. Treasury who were calling the shots, you have to understand that Rubin, in turn, was listening to the behind-the-scenes voices of the capital market vigilantes. Call it bailing out Wall Street if you like, but future capital infusions into Mexico by the private sector would have been impossible without the loans and guarantees offered by the U.S. Treasury. The vigilantes were in control.

Similarly, well-publicized financial confrontations around the globe, such as those in Argentina, France, Italy, and Spain in recent years, all serve as reminders of the power of the vigilantes. But it's the implicit rather than the explicit discipline they enforce that is perhaps most important. In order to attract capital to compete in today's worldwide marketplace, every country has to offer an attractive package that entices potential investors. Nations today are in competition with one another to win the fancy of the vigilantes. Some might wonder why so many governments have suddenly caught the old-time religion of balanced budgets and fiscal discipline—including the U.S. government. Could it be that Newt Gingrich is simply smarter than his predecessors Tip O'Neill and Tom

Foley? Not likely. When he and other Republican congressmen and -women were elected to shift government policies in the direction of a free-market economy, and when President Clinton recognized the same mood and shifted his policies toward a decidedly more conservative bent, the voters may not have realized it, but they were all responding to the policies of the capital market vigilantes in order to strengthen the U.S. economy and provide job security for themselves into the twenty-first century.

ECONOMICS 101
Fiscal and Monetary Policy

Modern-day governments perform many functions, but two of the most important are establishing budgets and controlling the supply of money. *Fiscal policy* refers to a government's budget and whether it is operating in surplus or running a deficit. If a government is said to have fiscal discipline, it means that it is close to balancing its budget or at least is moving substantially in that direction.

Monetary policy refers to the policies of a government's central bank (such as our Federal Reserve) that affect the amount of money and bank reserves in circulation. An easy monetary policy is generally associated with rapid increases in the amount of money supply and the reserves that back it. "Tight money" refers to slow growth in the money supply and the high real interest rates that usually accompany such policies.

Central banks the world around are under similar pressure. When tight monetary policies and high real interest rates are lacking, the vigilantes can and do attack on the "wires" by selling and depreciating currencies. Within a few months of such an assault, domestic inflation rates begin to rise, reducing the attractiveness of local bond and stock markets and thus the ability of the nation to compete for new capital. The attacks begin a vicious cycle in which the perceived looseness of monetary policy eventually leads to relative economic weakness and ultimate stagnation. Because these conditions make it harder for politicians to get reelected, they usually support the central bank disciplines, unlike in prior decades, when such policies might have been cause for their condemnation or political attacks.

These right turns toward fiscal and monetary discipline are, of course, a bond- and stockholder's dream because they reinforce the trend toward lower inflation. My 2 percent inflation forecast for the balance of the century is due in no small part to the ability of the vigilantes to influence the outcome. There are, however, some negatives to all of this. Vigilantes ride fast horses, and when they decide to move, their trail becomes obvious almost overnight. Because they move so quickly, often in unison, all markets have become much more volatile in the short term, which causes not only some sleepless nights for investors but financial calamity for some who refuse to recognize the situation. The financial collapse of Orange County, California, in early 1995 was perhaps the most visible example. As the vigilantes ran for the hills in the U.S. bond market in 1994, fearing strong economic growth and higher inflation, they forced this highly leveraged California county (I live right in the center of it) to declare bankruptcy. Reporters subsequently discovered that County Treasurer Robert Citron had invested heavily in high-risk, complex derivative securities that were probably inappropriate for a municipal government account. The ironic part of the story is that nine months later, Orange County would have been as prosperous as ever. Almost at the same instant as the bankruptcy declaration, the vigilantes changed direction and initiated a stunning bull market with sharply higher prices and lower yields that would have returned Orange County's portfolio to clover later that year.

Strategic Implications

The influence of the vigilantes and the increased volatility in their wake produce two major strategic effects. First of all, this volatility, as described later in this book (Chapter 9), has economic bounds. Capital market vigilantes can move markets quickly, but they can't always take them wherever they want them to go. If interest rates move too high, the domestic and world economies push back. If they go too low, inflation rears its head. An investor needs an educated idea as to just what interest rates on the high and low sides will constrain overexuberant vigilantes. I believe these yields to be 5 percent and 7 percent for long-term U.S. Treasury rates. Don't be disturbed by volatile movement within that range. *But, when yields edge close to 7 percent, it should be viewed as a buying opportunity; when they drop to 5 percent, you should think about selling.* Everything in between will be due to normal business cycle fluctuation and to "noise" generated by the vigilantes themselves.

THE SAVVY IVESTOR:
Market Timing

There are few topics in the area of investing more controversial than market timing. When Financier J. Pierpont Morgan was asked what the stock market was going to do, he replied, "It will fluctuate," and that about sums up the frustrations of most investors. To be able to time the moves of the market and so consistently buy low and sell high ranks with the dreams of Ponce de León.

The difficulty as I see it, though, has to do with an investor's time frame and not necessarily with his or her intelligence or industriousness. If you try to time the market on a *short-term* basis, human emotion begins to play tricks with your senses and intellect. In addition, economic and business statistics over the short term can be quite random, which inhibits the formation of one-way market trends that can be either bought or sold. Still, an investor must attempt to time his investment. Even the Bible advises that "To everything there is a season." To do it successfully, though, you have to turn, turn, turn to a *longer-term* outlook. Focus your mental acumen on what will happen over the next three to five years instead of the next three to five weeks or months. Over the longer term, genuine, meaningful trends emerge that may be tracked objectively. Your chances of success will improve immeasurably!

A second observation has to do with the business cycle timing attempted by market professionals within the context of today's vigilante activity. In the last few years, market behavior has become more and more anticipatory. *Front-running* is probably a more descriptive word. Each vigilante on his or her own has been trying to beat the other vigilantes to the punch. Whereas in the past it paid to wait for statistical confirmation about the onset of a recession or the certainty of a recovery, now the markets may have made the bulk of their moves before either begins. In September 1995, for example, long-term Treasuries had declined 1½ percent, or 150 basis points, from their peak simply on the basis of a growth slowdown. The preceding bear market of 1994 was overblown as well, partially because

E C O N O M I C S   1 0 1
The Business Cycle

If economies grew in a regular, uninterrupted fashion, there'd be no need to discuss the business cycle. However, business has grown in a curiously uneven path for centuries with periods of above-average advance known as *recoveries* and (usually) shorter periods of decline labeled *recessions*. This regular, wavelike course is known as the *business cycle*.

In addition, economists have found other types of cycles. The standard business cycle described in the financial press tends to be three to five years in length from peak to peak, but longer-term cycles, such as the Kondratieff wave, theoretically produced by cycles of technological innovation, may encompass up to fifty years.

All of them are important to investors because they affect interest rates, profits, and the prices of securities themselves. Being able to locate the current point of the business cycle, for instance, can provide entry and exit points for longer-term market-timing decisions.

What causes these cycles? There are hundreds of rational explanations, ranging from monetary and fiscal policy to fluctuations in the animal spirits of capitalists themselves.

of the vigilantes' tendency to yell "Fire!" and then rush for the exits ahead of their friends in the adjoining seats. Appropriate timing, then, as it relates to stock and bond market business cycle analysis, may have to be adjusted in the future for the "vigilante effect." Timing the market on a short-term basis is always a difficult proposition, but those that try it must recognize the power of the vigilantes and enter or exit the market earlier than in prior economic cycles.

There are lots of hunters out in them thar woods, and only a few golden eggs to find. While it's easy to be a genius in a bull market, the Butler Creek environment will require a long-term secular view that takes heed of the vigilantes. They're going to help to slow nominal growth and keep inflation low, but the markets will bounce more because of them. Good hunting to you!

FIVE

The Plankton Theory

Boomers, Busters, and the Future of Growth

When I was twenty-two, I came face to face with a Marine drill sergeant who turned out to be the meanest old dog you'd never want to meet in your life. Sergeant Cruz was his name, but "Sir" was the only title he recognized—and that at a minimum of 110 decibels from a squeaky-voiced kid barely able to shave. I was never cut out to be a military man—and Sergeant Cruz knew it. Like a lion instinctively culling out the weakest wildebeest from the herd, he picked me out the moment I took that fateful first step inside the Pensacola barracks in October 1966. In the first ten minutes, my hair was gone; during the next ten, my body became vulnerable; and by sundown my ego was completely destroyed. I wanted to be a Vietnam jet jockey, but my commitment was weak and the sergeant smelled it almost instinctively. "Where are your *LOVE* beads, mister?" he would scream in my face. "In San Francisco, SIR!" became my accepted reply. "Well, then, you'd better get your hairy —— out of here and back to your hometown real soon, don't you think, boy?" "No, SIR!" I would squeak in return.

Ah, Sergeant Cruz. Everyone else hated him too. He was the

personification of the system we were being forced to adapt to within the short span of twelve weeks. After that, we hoped, we would be officers and learning the insides of a cockpit instead of a latrine. But Cruz was standing in our way—especially mine, it seemed. I could do nothing right. I stayed awake until three in the morning searching for the microscopic piece of rust in my rifle that he always seemed to find during inspection. I never slept in my bunk, because the hospital corners he demanded for my sheets took more than an hour to make, and there was simply no time. All the while, my broken body, though never once touched by his hand, was in agony from the countless marches, push-ups, pull-ups, obstacle runs, and anything else that you've seen in the movies and thought was pure Hollywood fiction. I'm here to tell you—all those stories are true. "You'll never fly a jet, Mr. Gross!" he would scream. "BLIMPS are more your style!" He was right, as it turned out, but the Navy wasn't using blimps in Vietnam, so I eventually found my home on a destroyer in the South Pacific. I'll never forget Sergeant Cruz, though. My twelve weeks with him were three months from hell, but they were my first big steps on the way to manhood.

As was customary at the commissioning ceremony for young officers, each new ensign signed a dollar bill and handed it to his drill sergeant in the hope of being remembered once he became famous down the road. I didn't know it then, but I realize now that it was Sergeant Cruz who should have done the signing. Bill Gross and a thousand other blimp pilots have surely disappeared from his memory banks, but Marine Sergeant Alfredo Cruz will remain in ours, with the highest respect and esteem, for the rest of our lives.

The Plankton Theory

Sergeant Cruz believed in survival of the fittest. Almost instinctively he culled out the weak so that only the strong would survive as Navy jet pilots. Survival in the financial markets is equally demanding. If you fall asleep in the cockpit as you pilot your portfolio through turbulent skies, there may be a crash in your financial future. So you must be vigilant, even if, you turn over your portfolio to a mutual fund manager like me. At the very least, you still need to decide whether to invest in stocks, bonds, or cash. For that, it's helpful to understand a bit more about the science of demographics, and to help you do that, I'm going to introduce my own dictum, known as the Plankton Theory.

The Plankton Theory, like life itself, begins in the ocean. Plankton, of course, are the almost microscopic organisms that serve as food for higher aquatic life forms. Without plankton, most fish and mammals in the sea could not survive, since most species depend on other fish for their existence and plankton are the initial building blocks of the entire process. Logic would suggest, therefore, that in attempting to forecast the well-being of the Great White Whale, Jaws, or even Jaws II, one of the factors to consider would be the status and future outlook of the plankton. That, in a nutshell, is the Plankton Theory.

What possible significance could this have for the investment world? Plenty. Take, for example, the area of real estate, especially that of single-family housing. We're all familiar with the rapid escalation of home prices that occurred in the United States between 1975 and 1985. For most Americans, their homes were the best and in many cases the only investment they made in their entire lives. Some went so far as to invest in several homes and endured a "negative carry" on the cash flow in anticipation of enormous capital gains a few years down the road. In other words, after purchasing that second or third home and leasing it to other people, they received rent insufficient to cover the cost of their interest payments—they had a negative carry. Still, the resale value of their investments soared for nearly a decade, making the ploy profitable in the long run. Then the trend turned the other way. Over the past decade, real estate values have grown slowly or not at all. How does one explain this?

One way might be via the Plankton Theory. In the case of real estate, the plankton would be the first-time buyer, perhaps a young married couple with a desire to own their own home but very little capital to carry it off. When the time comes that they *can't* pull it off, through an inability either to come up with a down payment or to service the monthly mortgage, the plankton would disappear and the escalation in housing prices would ease as well. For, unless the current homeowner has someone to sell *his* house to, he'll be unable to afford the house with the nicer view or the extra bedroom, and the process will continue higher and higher into the pricey echelons of Beverly Hills and Shaker Heights. In the end, the entire market will wither on the investment vine, and home prices will stop increasing at a rapid rate. So, to gauge the overall health of the housing market, look first at the plankton: the people who are moving in at the bottom of the economic food chain. Without their presence and financial vitality, the real estate market's not going to resume its upward path anytime soon.

Follow Those Boomers

In fact, while markets consist of millions upon millions of people making countless independent decisions, when taken as a whole they can be combined into the quantitative sociological science we know as demographics. Demographics is the analysis of population flows. Its statistics describe how many people were born in a certain year and how many people are likely to die in particular years in the future. Among other things, it can offer a very specific, highly accurate picture of who's alive now and who's likely to be alive twenty years from now. Aside from a natural catastrophe or world war, about the only variables that could change things a lot would be future birthrates or immigration patterns, and those tend to be relatively constant over a short period of time.

I've often said that if I had to go off to a South Sea island without any source of communication for the next few years, the one thing I'd want to know when it came to structuring my investment portfolio before departing would be demographics. Individual plankton, when combined in a unified mass, can move markets, and it's not just the housing market I'm talking about. Long-term price trends for both stocks and bonds are *dominated* by demographics, and this is where I would turn first, whether on an island or not, in forecasting the future of either.

THE SAVVY INVESTOR:
Fundamental Versus Technical Analysis

There are two methods money managers use to forecast the markets, and, like oil and water, they usually don't mix. I'm referring to *fundamental* and *technical analysis.*

Fundamental analysis refers to the use of such factors as corporate balance sheets and income statements to forecast future price movements of stocks and bonds. Fundamental analysts (including the overwhelming majority of managers on Wall Street) also consider past records of and future prospects for such things as corporate sales, earnings, and the quality of management in assessing the outlook for various stocks and corporate bonds. Demographic factors, to the extent that they affect economic and corporate performance, would be important to a fundamentalist.

Technical analysts are the witch doctors of our business. By deciphering stock price movement patterns and volume changes, these Merlins believe they can forecast the future. Human nature, they believe, is depicted in their historical stock charts. Patterns of greed, fear, or simply "getting even" show up time and time again, they believe, and certain stock chart patterns can tip off investors when to buy or sell. If you thought "head and shoulders" was just a shampoo, you need to bone up on technical analysis. (To a technician, a head-and-shoulders pattern is a three-peak stock price movement, supposed to have predictive significance for future price changes.) Me? Well, there's something to it, I'll admit, but I've been using Prell for years!

Demographics has been spiced up over the past half century by a group we know in the United States as the "baby boomers," born between 1945 and the early 1960s. Children of the veterans of World War II, they were a reflection not only of society's instinctive need to replace its war dead but of the postwar prosperity that made new and growing families possible. That second qualifier is important; Europe and Japan do not have boomers as we do, primarily because they couldn't afford to have children at the same rates we could due to their decimated economies.

The boomers have spiced things up simply because there are so many of them. They have a big club, and whenever they decide to swing, an investor had better pay attention. *Lots* of plankton here. Let's take a look at this boom in Figure 5-1.

This graphic shows the tremendous surge of births that took place during the years between 1946 and the early 1960s, as well as the "baby bust" that followed in the 1970s. These patterns are the reason why there are "boomers" (forty-somethings) and "busters" (twenty-somethings) in 1996. The boomers have been important because of their sheer numbers, not only to the economy but to the in-

FIGURE 5-1.
NUMBER OF LIVE BIRTHS, IN MILLIONS, 1909–1993

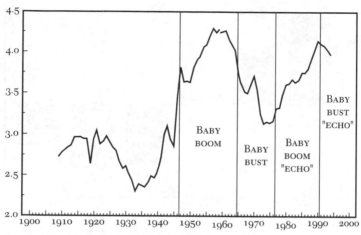

Sources: National Center for Health Statistics; DL| Demographics.

vestment markets as well. In the 1970s and early '80s, for instance, it was possible to trace any number of trends to the fact that the boomers were coming of age and beginning to borrow and spend money at a very rapid rate. If you thought Jimmy Carter was solely responsible for double-digit inflation, think again. If you thought OPEC and skyrocketing oil prices were purely a geopolitical phenomenon, think again. If you thought the real estate frenzy and the ensuing savings and loan debacle were just part of the "decade of greed," think again. All these phenomena are significantly related to the boomers and the fact that Americans in their mid-twenties began to spend money quickly. Take a look at another demographic chart (Figure 5-2).

Each bar in this graph represents the average spending increase (decrease) for individual consumers in various decades of their lives. The twenty-fifth-year bar, for instance, reflects individuals at the median point for the twenty- to thirty-year-old group. The graph shows that U.S. consumers between twenty and forty tend to increase their spending at enormous rates—they spend $12,000 more per year as twenty-somethings than as teenagers and $8,000 more at

FIGURE 5-2.
CHANGE IN AVERAGE ANNUAL CONSUMER
EXPENDITURE THROUGH AGING (DOLLARS)

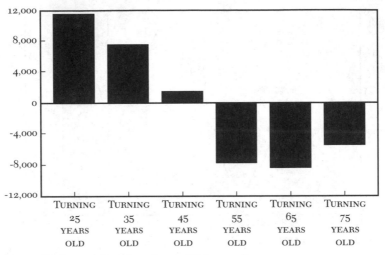

Sources: 1990 Consumer Expenditure Survey; DLJ Demographics.

thirty-five than in their twenties. After that, expenditures fall (and savings rise) for those older than fifty. But the important point of both the previous charts is that the boomers were twenty to thirty years old during the fifteen-year period from 1970 to 1985, and it was their spending that caused booms in many segments of the economy. When they bought their first houses in their late twenties, U.S. housing starts soared past 2 million per year. Their desire for homes caused housing prices to skyrocket to 20 to 30 percent annual rates. Not only that, they also bought furniture, appliances, and TVs—almost all on credit. They were like a hoard of locusts descending on the Kansas plains. One year, there were low inflation and cheap housing; five years later, inflation was at 13 percent and most homes were priced in the six digits. This was not a Jimmy Carter phenomenon or a Democratic-versus-Republican issue. There were just a lot of boomers in need of places to settle down.

Busting the Consumption Parade

Now, let's look at the "busters" who followed. These bambini were born between 1965 and 1975, in the wake of the previous boom. Demographics tells us that there were a lot fewer of them—about a million per year fewer on average. By projecting their age group forward, we find that the busters are reaching their prime purchasing years in the 1990s. Wow! Given the busters' scanty numbers, can it be any surprise that housing starts are down from 2 million to 1.3 million per year, that housing prices are flat or lower (especially in California), and that inflation is at its lowest level since—well, since the boomers grew up? See why the plankton are so important and why demographics is the first thing I want to know before I make an investment decision?

Now let's update this phenomenon and pretend that you and I are going off to our individual South Sea islands (we'll correspond by floating messages back and forth in bottles) for the next two to three years. It's easy to see that not much is going to change between now and the beginning of the twenty-first century. The busters will still be heading the consumption parade, and consumption as well as housing is going to be weak because there are so few of them. Since housing and consumption of goods and services, when taken together, add up to 70 percent–plus of our total GDP, it's going to be very difficult for the economy to generate strong economic growth. That suggests relatively low inflation, attractive bond returns, and okay but not super potential for stocks.

One of the reasons I think stocks might still do all right in a period of slow economic growth has to do with the boomers again. The boomers are now in their saving years, and these days, that means mutual funds instead of bank deposits at 4 percent. If boomers are going to be buying mutual funds, stock funds will be a popular choice, at least for a while, and there's lots of buying power in the stock market—lots of plankton. So I wouldn't count out stocks even in the face of a moderate economy. Still, 8 percent returns are about all you can expect. There aren't enough plankton out there buying *things,* and in the final analysis the strength of corporate sales and profits, not savings flows, is what drives stock prices. If corporate profit growth slows down, baby-boomer savers are more likely to increase their purchases of bonds or invest more of their savings in the more attractive foreign markets.

Slowing Down the World Around

One last piece of demographic minutiae: it's a global economy these days, and you might just be wondering if the same conditions apply to other major economic powers. I've mentioned the fact that on a per capita basis there weren't as many babies born in Japan and Europe as there were in the United States following World War II. The people there simply couldn't afford them. Consequently, they didn't experience the same type of housing boom nor the dramatic inflation rates we had in the 1970s and '80s. But the interesting thing, as Figure 5-3 shows, is that their "bust" is just as bad as or worse than ours.

FIGURE 5-3.
DEVELOPED COUNTRIES, POPULATION CHANGE
BY AGE GROUPS, 1991–2000 (MILLIONS OF
PERSONS)

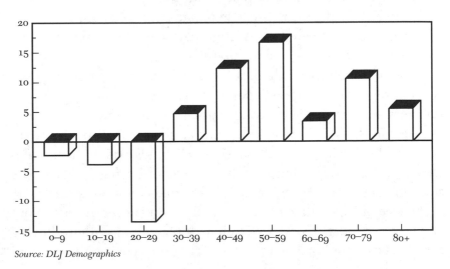

Source: DLJ Demographics

The entire developed world is winding its way through the 1990s with 15 million fewer prime consumers than in the 1980s. Of that 15 million, the United States accounts for a loss of 5 million and Japan and Europe for shrinkage of 10 million people. Both Japan and Europe, as a matter of fact, have a substantially older population base than we do, which means more saving and less consumption than here. So the demographics of the industrialized world are simply stinko when it comes to future economic growth. Without the emerging nations, which have very *young* populations, the world economy would be in dire shape indeed.

Don't look for any help from our trading partners in Japan and Europe when it comes to demographic spending power. If anything, they'll be a drag, helping to keep economic growth and inflation low through the balance of the century.

SIX

Einsteinian Economics

The Secular Trend Toward Lower Wages

"Ghost of the future!" Scrooge exclaimed. "I fear you more than any Spectre I have seen."

Charles Dickens, *A Christmas Carol*

One of my favorite "reflective" books is *A Christmas Carol* by Charles Dickens. His story, of course, is universal and can be appreciated by Christian, Jew, and Moslem alike. It is centered around Christmas, but is not about Christmas, and is, at its essence, a parable of the renewal of the human spirit, a tale that teaches us that anyone—even an Ebenezer Scrooge—can change. Confronted by the Ghost of Christmas Future, Scrooge is shown his own corpse as he "lay in the dark empty house with not a man, a woman or a child, to say that [he] had been kind" to them in any way. We must love one another, Dickens beseeches, or die unloved, and through Scrooge we rediscover that potential for ourselves and all humanity.

Throughout the story, Dickens uses the device of ghosts that Scrooge truly believes he is experiencing—this is no dream as far as Ebenezer is concerned—but it's the third ghost he fears the most and which forces Scrooge to mend his ways. This "draped and hooded" specter is the inevitable face of death for Scrooge and for us all, and by facing its horror, he ultimately salvages the remainder of his life.

An altogether brilliant lesson, in my opinion. Because we are unsure of when we will die, we view life as an inevitable continuum, disturbed only by infrequent reminders of mortality that are quickly repressed. "Hospitals and funerals are for other people, not us," our egos whisper, and we behave as if it were true. Flowers go unsmelled, roads go untaken, loved ones go unhugged. How fortunate Scrooge was to have met his third ghost while he was still alive.

But confronting the masque of death straight on is, I suppose, a dangerous task. Much like looking at a blazing noontime sun, it can destroy, not enrich, life's wonders if the specter becomes an obsession instead of a warning. Scrooge needed only a midnight's worth of horror to turn his life around. But most of us mortals may need more than that. Life's tragedies occur everywhere, all the time, and at a minimum, a series of quick, brief meaningful glances can help us all to become more like the Ebenezer of Christmas Day instead of the Scrooge of Christmas Eve. While at fifty-two I'm nowhere near as vulnerable as I hope to be at eighty-two, I'm beginning to find that it helps to mentally project my life's wave moving ever and ever closer to shore and to envision the reality of its crashing one day into earthly oblivion. I see the foam absorbed quickly by the porous sand, but the water itself recedes back into the larger, seemingly infinite mass behind. It's then that I realize that you and I are not individual waves, but part of an ocean—all of us traveling toward the same shore but oblivious most of the time to our common humanity. That's what Scrooge came to understand from his Ghost of Christmas Future. May God help us all to see that light.

❖   ❖   ❖

History, according to Karl Marx, was economics in action. Change the dynamics of an economy, and you could change history itself. His disciples—Lenin, Stalin, Mao Tse-tung—proved his point during much of the twentieth century, but the changes wrought by capitalism since its birth in the seventeenth century have been even more dramatic. The Industrial Revolution, for instance, helped produce democracy, the near evaporation of agrarian society, the birth of modern cities, feminism, and arguably the slow decline of religion and traditional morality in Western society itself. If this seems a little vague or even farfetched, consider what has happened in the space of your own lifetime. Since around 1970, a decline in U.S. productivity brought about by low savings rates, excessive defense spending, and an extension of the modern welfare state has led to a decline in real wages that has forced women out of the home and into the workplace. The nuclear family of Ward and June Cleaver is but one of the casualties, and America's social disintegration since then can, in part, be laid at the feet of a sputtering economic engine.

Still, all of humanity's historical and societal evolution cannot be attributed to economics alone (dismal science that it is). Other factors, including certain scientists and scientific theories, have lent a helping hand as well. Charles Darwin, for instance, turned the Old Testament's Book of Genesis on its head and, in the view of many, hastened the advent of moral relativism. Einstein and Freud did much the same thing when they stated that life's and nature's laws weren't always what they appear to be on the surface. Centuries-old theories of physics were replaced with Einstein's concepts of relativity, and no longer could we proclaim with certainty that Newton's apple would fall to earth. Einstein could conceive of just the reverse: the earth rising to meet the apple. These scientific advances were important not just because of the economic developments they helped cause (atomic energy, for one) but because of their indirect influence on societal mores and attitudes as well. For instance, Paul Johnson, in his seminal book *Modern Times,* attributes the rise of Stalin and Hitler partly to the gradual inculcation of "relativist" scientific concepts into the behavior patterns of society as a whole. Similarly, today's theories of advanced physics, which describe the random behavior of subatomic particles, and the trend of present-day genetics to attribute many individual psychological and physical maladies to heredity as opposed to behavior, may be partly responsible for the breakdown of individual responsibility and the slow but persistent spread of cultural decay so many of us perceive in Western societies.

Thus, today's self-centered society with its related vices—crime, illegitimacy, and child neglect—may be exacerbated by the spread of particular scientific theories. If Charles Murray's *The Bell Curve* is right and genetics is mainly responsible for differences in IQ, does this weaken individuals' motivation to take responsibility for their own lives? If human emotions are chemically determined—if how we feel on any particular day is merely a function of a certain mix of hormones sending signals to the brain—where's our need or even ability to assume conscious control of our emotions and reactions? You may think this is a stretch—that those committing crimes and abandoning families know little of these scientific theories—but the moral message they imply is communicated in numerous ways. Nike's ad campaign—"Just do it"—exalts action, not thinking, and is reflective of what well-educated advertising executives, not just high school dropouts, believe their world looks like. Movies reflect the culture in much the same way. Hollywood's current fixation on violence is geared to sell tickets, yes, but why now instead of twenty years ago? In part, it's because writers and directors have absorbed the randomness and hopelessness that advanced scientific theory seems to point toward and have incorporated the conclusions into their films.

These musings are meant to point to explanations for historical and societal changes that lie beneath the visible and readily apparent surface of events. When you hear comments such as "People don't seem to care anymore," it's important to consider *why* that might be true. Even explanations such as "a breakdown in our institutions" or the "decline of religion" are but superficial excuses. What *caused* them to disintegrate? More often than not, the explanation can be found in economic and scientific developments, some for the better, some for the worse, but always influential in terms of how we function as individuals within a society.

Waging a Losing Battle

The economic forces that have led to the breakup of the American family and strengthened the phenomenon of the two-wage household remain as strong as ever in the late 1990s: U.S. savings rates are low; our currency, despite some recent strength, remains in a gradual long-term downtrend; and perhaps most important, the ability of U.S. corporations to outsource production to low-wage nations is a continuing damper on labor's bargaining powers and the strength of the union movement, both here and abroad. Even with the recent resurgence of U.S. productivity, wages haven't benefited. Former Labor Secretary Robert Reich declares that productivity improvements are going into corporate profits, not workers' pockets, and he appears to be right. The Commerce Department chart in Figure 6-1, shows a decided downward trend in wages and salaries as a percentage of corporate output over the past forty years. Total compensation, which includes pension and medical benefits, has been flat over the same period but has shown a decline of 5 percent since the early 1970s and a drop of 2 to 3 percent over the past several years—a trend that underscores Reich's comments.

What has been the cause of this deterioration in labor's share of the country's wealth, and what significance does it have for investors? There's never only one reason for any secular movement,

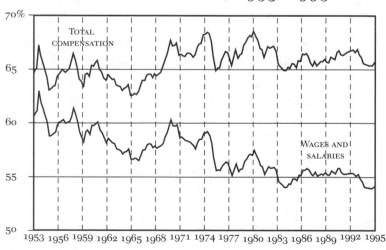

FIGURE 6-1.
LABOR'S SHARE AS A PERCENTAGE OF
NATIONAL OUTPUT, 1953–1995

Source: U.S. Department of Commerce.

but there are several strong explanations that deserve an airing. With the near-simultaneous fall of the Berlin Wall, the liberalization of worldwide trade policies, and the globalization of capital markets, *labor in the 1990s has become a fungible commodity.* Time was, back in those "I like Ike" days of the 1950s, when automobiles, to use one example, had to be built in Detroit. If you didn't belong to a union or live in Michigan, you wouldn't be working on a Chrysler assembly line. The ability of labor to institute what was then known as "cost-push" inflation was significant, simply because there was nowhere else for capital to go. The fall of the Wall in 1989 accelerated changes in this picture that were already taking place. Free-trade policies and globalized capital markets have made it possible for businesses to set up shop almost anywhere, making virtually anything. Many of the high-paying manufacturing jobs in the United States have simply departed to other countries, replaced by lower-paying, often minimum-wage, service-oriented jobs. The result has been an increase in prosperity on a global basis but also what we now recognize as a bifurcation of labor—a separation of the haves from the have-nots with a diminution of the American middle class as we once knew it.

Due to this decline in real wages, the United States is now very competitive with other trading partners in the industrialized world. In addition to wages and the dollar being relatively lower, our productivity is even higher due to our extensive use of new technologies, ranging from computers to telecommunications. Table 6-1 points this out in spades—"We're number one . . ."

This competitiveness, though, has come largely at the expense of labor. Corporate downsizing, the use of technology to displace employees, and the economies of scale produced by mergers and acquisitions have all contributed to keeping a lid on wages. When Chase Manhattan merged with Chemical Bank in 1995, for instance, 12,000 layoffs were immediately announced, which helped further spread the now-pervasive fear that corporate CEOs had the whip and could crack it at a moment's notice. That type of fear keeps both unions and the demands of nonunionized workers in check, and it's no small reason why stockholders are profiting at the expense of employees.

TABLE 6-1.
WORLD COMPETITIVENESS: THE TOP 20

1.	United States of America	11.	Taiwan
2.	Singapore	12.	Canada
3.	Hong Kong	13.	Austria
4.	Japan	14.	Australia
5.	Switzerland	15.	Sweden
6.	Germany	16.	Finland
7.	Netherlands	17.	France
8.	New Zealand	18.	United Kingdom
9.	Denmark	19.	Belgium/ Luxembourg
10.	Norway	20.	Chile

Source: *International Institute for Management Development.*

It's not, however, just blue-collar workers who are suffering. Most of the headlines have emphasized the effect on lower- and middle-class workers, with the suggestion that the highly educated and the wealthy stand to benefit from their anguish. Perhaps that is so if you own lots of financial assets such as stocks and bonds, but almost all highly educated upper-class Americans are in a similar, although somewhat more secure, lifeboat. The pilots, engineers, lawyers, and doctors of this country are feeling the ramifications of globalization as well—their standards of living are suffering, and their ability to raise their own wages or compensation is limited. The invisible hand of Adam Smith is working on almost all Americans.

The Global Vise

Why is this so? How can doctors in Philadelphia be affected by cheap labor in Bangladesh? If there was ever a "product" that was purely "local," you'd think it would be medicine. *The fact is that globalized trade and freewheeling international capital markets have placed nations themselves in competition with one another.* Ever since the days of mercantilism in the 1700s, of course, competition among nations has existed, but in the 1990s free trade has accentuated the battle. For the United States to maintain its economic standing among nations, it must institute policies that keep inflation low, maintain a relatively stable currency, and encourage high rates of investment. One big economic step in the direction of *all three* of those requirements is to balance the federal budget—or at least reduce the budget deficit below that of the United States' major trading partners. Doing that, of course, requires hard choices, the brunt of which is now being borne by the Republican Congress. In 1994, Hillary-care was rejected, and one year later spending on Medicare and Medicaid were under attack.

Now *not only government but private industry is waging the battle to contain costs and remain competitive in a global environment.* The HMOs that doctors abhor were a creation not of the federal bureaucracy but of the private sector. With both government and corporate purchasers of health care refusing to pay escalating costs for medical care, it's no wonder that doctors are now suffering casualties in a battle they hardly recognize and may not understand. They are not the only white-collar professionals who will be affected. For instance, the limited financial resources brought about by global competition spell an end to the growth of teachers' and professors' salaries. Tuition, which constitutes a good portion of the total expense of college, cannot rise at double-digit rates as it has over the past ten years or so. The crunch is even starting to hit professional sports. The prolonged baseball strike of 1994–1995 reflected the new reality that owners, fans, and television networks cannot continue to pay $3 million annual salaries for mediocre talents or perhaps even stars. We are retreating from the heady days when athletes could demand any price for the ability to hit a ball with a wooden bat.

I've taken a while to make my point, I suppose, and raised a few others along the way. The main concept is this: no job or profession today is impervious to the effects of global free trade. Whereas economists have tended to focus on the bifurcation of labor and distinguish between the uneducated have-nots and the technologically astute haves, there should be an increasing realization that globalization affects us all: pilots, doctors, investment managers, even those who've retired and expect continuing health care and Social Security benefits via government largesse. Those days are disappearing. While the negatives show up in the form of job insecurity and reductions in salaries and benefits, there are economic positives in the form of reduced wage pressure, low inflation, and a general increase in U.S. and worldwide prosperity. Creative destruction is what capitalism is all about, and all of us—doctor, lawyer, Indian chief—will be faced with the challenge of the current phase of capitalist change for some years to come.

Fighting Back

Can anything be done to reverse this trend? It's interesting to hark back to the early part of the twentieth century—to the days of Henry Ford and his revolutionary "$5" solution. Ford decreed that he was going to nearly double wages at his Detroit auto factory to the then-unthinkable level of $5 a day, so that his workers could afford to buy their own product. It was a startling announcement, though Ford was following the theory of a nineteenth-century economist, J.-B. Say, who had developed a theory later labeled "Say's Law," stating, in effect, that supply creates its own demand. Ford was thus not being unreasonably benevolent. Productivity gains due to the innovation of the assembly line were enormous, and he could more than afford to pass on a part of those gains in the form of higher wages and still have plenty left over for himself. A repetition of Ford's gambit, however, seems impossible in the global economic environment of the 1990s. Can you imagine a dominant computer, semiconductor, or software company initiating a similar strategy today? It would be quickly outmaneuvered by competitors who would have the ability to lower product *prices,* not raise *wages,* in the face of their competitor's folly.

So the Ford solution appears to be out. Robert Reich and Bill Clinton, of course, have tried a similar "$5" tactic from the government side by increasing the minimum wage, with results so far unknown. Their attempts to increase workers' access to high-tech, high-paying jobs via training and education are long-term in nature and seem to stress action by the public sector, which probably hampers their effectiveness. Real wages can temporarily be improved by raising trade barriers and increasing tariffs—at least according to labor unions and the Pat Buchanans of the world—but that dubious solution is not in the political cards over the next few years. Neither is a significant tax cut for lower- and middle-class Americans, which would improve their *after-tax* wages.

ECONOMICS 101
Free Trade Versus Protectionism

While the overall benefits of international free trade when contrasted with protectionism are rarely disputed, some individuals and groups benefit more than others. Almost everyone, for instance, benefits when U.S.-made computers can be exchanged for Middle Eastern oil or Chinese soft goods, but there is increasing evidence that corporations (capital) may gain an additional advantage over labor (wages) in the process. When U.S. manufacturers can increase production in foreign countries with cheaper labor, high-paying jobs are at least temporarily exported and the cheaper wages of foreigners are imported as U.S. wage earners lose the leverage to demand salary increases. That, of course, is positive for corporate profits and helps to keep inflation low, but it may be a primary reason for the paltry growth in U.S. real wages over the past decade. The remedy is not to throw up trade barriers à la Pat Buchanan but to compensate the afflicted end of the labor market with lower or no taxes.

Perhaps it's not enough to discuss the nature of our predicament and its effects on the bond market without offering some advice of my own as to how we might get out of it. It's easy to slam the politicians, I suppose, and suggest that real revolutions begin from within the community, but my or anyone else's "thousand points of light" may not be enough to bridge the broadening chasm between the "upper" and "under" classes. Is there anything the government can do to rectify the solution at least partially?

I'm dubious about the Clinton minimum wage/training approach. Government doesn't know how to run a railroad, let alone an economy. It's almost always best to let market forces channel capital to the most productive areas and keep the bureaucrats out of it. After all, that is what we've learned from the fall of the Soviet empire, as well as the continuing troubles of the socialist governments in Western Europe.

Pat Buchanan and the Republican Right, on the other hand, believe in trade barriers, tariffs, and walling off immigration in order to keep future jobs for American citizens. Nice try, Pat, but this is putrid economics, not just voodoo economics. You don't create prosperity by reducing trade or by increasing taxes, which is what a tariff is.

No, the only real government solution that incorporates the positives of a free-market economy while alleviating the plight of the bifurcated have-nots of our society would be to *eliminate* the taxes of all Americans earning less than, say, $25,000 a year. What could be simpler or more efficient and better rectify, in one giant step, the decline of the after-tax wages of the lower half of American society? Forget about a capital gains tax reduction; stockholders have more than their fair share already. Forget, too, about the "family tax" reduction offering a $500 credit for those with children. That's a Band-Aid, not a tourniquet. Republicans should zero in on the Democrats' political constituency and improve the plight of the bifurcated lower half, while staying true to their principles of free markets and lower taxes at the same time.

Aside from tax decreases for America's underclass, there may be little that can be done over the next few years to reduce the slow, steady deterioration of wages as a percentage of national output. Real inflation-adjusted wages may benefit somewhat if productivity gains continue their recent pace, but the outlook for labor is not good as long as corporations have the ability to move production overseas *and* as long as there are cheap, available foreign workers willing to produce at less than our minimum wage. That condition promises to persist at least through the early years of the twenty-first century.

What does all this mean for the nation, the economy, and in turn the investment markets? Well, in terms of America's future, it's not as simple as saying we're going to have to be content with working as hamburger flippers. We won't be. American democracy, as Tocqueville, Jefferson, and other political philosophers have pointed out, is a system in delicate balance. It depends on the general perception not of *equality* but of *equal opportunity*. Historically, we've addressed the grievances of the underprivileged with legislation that levels the playing field more completely than in any other nation. But today's problem is different. No piece of domestic legislation can level the *world* playing field, and the perception of equal opportunity is vanishing as a result. The complaints are numerous: We can't compete because the Japanese restrict our imports. We can't compete because India uses child labor. We can't compete because Mexico doesn't have the same environmental standards as we do. And so on. Opportunity is no longer equal on a *worldwide* basis, threatening our perception of a level playing field even within our own borders. American democracy is thus losing control of its economic destiny, causing frustration, discontent, violence, and the potential for class warfare. It is not a pretty picture nor a rosy forecast. Ultimately, our democracy itself may be threatened if authoritarian leadership is viewed as a solution.

The Secular Consequences of Low Wages

The fundamental economic and investment conclusion to be drawn from a prolonged weakness in the labor market is that consumption must languish as well. Personal income, which has driven increased consumption for decades, can no longer grow at a rate anywhere close to that seen in prior decades. And, low wage growth equals limited spending power. When you combine this secular phenomenon with record high levels of consumer debt (see Figure 6-2) and a demographic pattern in which the number of "twenty-somethings" is reduced and that of the high-savings population is increased over the

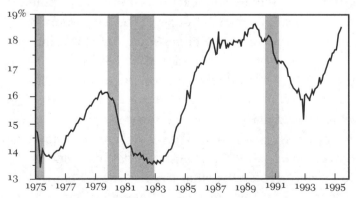

FIGURE 6-2.
CONSUMER INSTALLMENT CREDIT AS A SHARE
OF DISPOSABLE INCOME, 1975–1995

Note: Shaded areas represent recessions
Sources: Federal Reserve Board of Governors; U.S. Department of Commerce.

next five to ten years, you have a remarkable set of conditions that suggest—nay, almost mandate—low consumption growth over the same period.

These mega–economic forces, in combination with the efforts of the capital market vigilantes (see Chapter 3), have rarely, if ever, been in alignment as they are today. As a result, there is almost no ability to reinflate our domestic or world economy. The growth of consumption and retail sales in the United States will be anemic at best over the next several years; you should expect 3 percent on average. Nominal GDP growth will approximate 5 percent during the same period, and 2 percent inflation will soon become the norm in the United States, as it is around the globe at this very moment. As you can see in Figure 6-3, with the exception of Mexico and a few emerging nations, the overwhelming majority of countries are enjoying inflation rates as low as they've been in decades. This is no mystery.

Slow-growth soup will be the *plat du jour* for the balance of the

FIGURE 6-3.
CONSUMER PRICES PERCENTAGE CHANGE ON A YEAR EARLIER, 1995–1996

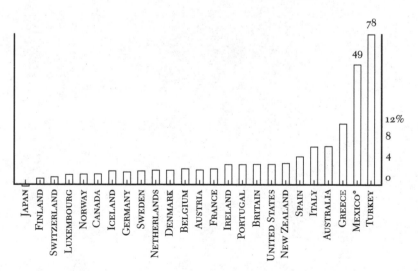

*Western.
Sources: OECD; national statistics

decade, and the economists and investment managers who seem concerned about an overly strong economy just don't get it. If you can't pump up wages, if you can't take on additional debt, and if the demographics point to savings, not consumption, there is almost no way out of this stagnant swamp.

So sit back and relax—as long as you have a well-paying job, that is. With 2 percent inflation, the U.S. and European bond markets are an attractive place to be for the foreseeable future. And while the history books may record that today's economic trends favored the rich over the poor, fostered an ever-widening gap in the standard of living among American citizens, and perhaps accelerated a continuing breakdown in U.S. society and its values, those with the capacity to save and invest must still be encouraged to take advantage of these glacial, inexorable trends. Societal solutions cannot easily be solved by Adam Smith's "invisible hand." For that we need to turn to family, religious institutions, and, in the last resort (yes, the *last* resort), government.

PART THREE

How to Invest in a 6 Percent World

SEVEN

The Pōpa and I

Resetting Your Investment Alarm Clock

I am a Father Guido Sarducci Catholic—which is to say, no Catholic at all. I earned my religious spurs and a three-year attendance pin at a Presbyterian Sunday school in Middletown, Ohio, but circumstances now find me appearing at a weekly Holy Mass in Laguna Beach, California, with my devout wife and less-than-reverent eight-year-old son, Nick. He told his mom while sandwiched between pews last week that if God could grant him one wish, it would be that he wouldn't have to go to church. I guess the Sarducci genes must run on his father's side of the family, but Nick's too young to smoke and doesn't quite have the Italian accent down yet.

I mention all of this because it's fortuitous sometimes to be an outsider on the inside, if only to objectively view a subjective and highly emotional topic such as religion and the Church. My weekly appearances at Saint Catherine's these past few years have put me into just such a position. I am aghast, for instance, at what Catholics *wear*. I know Laguna Beach is Surf City, U.S.A., but shorts and a T-shirt at church? Rarely if ever do you see men with even a sport coat and a tie, and the women are equally casual. And would you believe the altar boys wear Air Jordans? If this be their Sunday finest, our society has gone downhill faster than even I presumed. Sure,

Jesus wore sandals, but church is about respect, and to me it demeans the entire process of humbling yourself before God if you can't at least dress nicely in His presence.

Still, I must tell you, a Catholic Mass can be a moving ceremony, even for a part-time critic like me. To sing "Lamb of God, you take away the sins of the world" brings tears to my eyes each and every time. And if you want to feel the spirit of faith and community, repeat the Lord's Prayer and then shake hands with your fellow members of the congregation on all sides. "Peace be with you, peace be with you" is the mantra, and it's said with joy, hope, and a sincere desire that each soul in God's presence will find its own special solace. Nick likes to count the number of people he can shake hands with, and it's all we can do to keep him from walking up and down the aisle like an aspiring politician. "I got eleven today, Dad!" he crowed last Sunday, and I didn't know whether to laugh, cry, or submit his name in nomination.

Catholics have got a lot of other things right, too, and I mention this particularly in light of recent crime legislation that seems to point to fewer guns and more jails as a solution to the deplorable state of American society. I want those things, too, but they're simply Band-Aids over the fundamental wounds of our country brought about by the breakdown of the family and the lack of respect for institutions such as the Church. A recent *New York Times* article, however, cites a study purporting to explain why Catholic schools succeed, which may in turn say a lot about Catholicism itself. The answer in part is that the schools assume a high degree of moral authority and a strong sense of purpose. Teachers see themselves not so much as specialists in academic subjects as mentors and role models. Perhaps most important, the schools stress ideals of human dignity and caring along with a sense of community that many public schools seem to lack. I'm sure Catholic institutions aren't unique in this regard, but in an age when chaos reigns and politicians pass cheesy crime bills in an effort to prove they've gotten tough, it's heartening to know that America still has a moral foundation in its churches. Now, if those Catholics could ever start wearing proper slacks and shoes without "the pump," why, I might even quit smoking and stop talking with a phony Italian accent.

The Psychological "You"

Almost every time I step into Saint Catherine's, I experience a sense of inner quietude that leads to significant personal reflection. It's a good place to get to know yourself—as well as God, I suppose—and when it comes to the tangible world of investments, acknowledgment of both is not a bad idea. In this chapter, I'm going to stick to human, not holy, nature and discuss the psychological side of money management. Having laid the economic foundation in Part I, it's time to talk about *how* to go about investing in this brave new world of Butler Creek and the Era of 6 Percent.

There are several essentials in investing. Knowing what to do and how to navigate the tortuous tributaries of the financial world is certainly one of them. It would help every investor to have a thorough background in macroeconomic policy, as well as an intricate knowledge of the investment vehicles themselves—stocks, bonds, mutual funds, and so on. In addition, an up-to-date fact book on the fortunes of specific companies would be another basic requirement as you seek to row your boat down the investment rapids.

All these suggestions speak to the *what* portion of the investment equation, a topic that will be addressed further in the last few chapters of this book. But knowing what to do is not always enough. A race car driver who knows all the textbook procedures as his vehicle careens into a sideways four-wheel slide has still got to *execute* them to pull the car back onto the track—and the execution takes a delicate combination of timing, confidence, and raw nerve. Those elements can best be summarized as knowing *how* to do it, and the education in "how" can be as arduous and time-consuming as that in "what."

The "how" aspect of investing is psychological in nature. It is more subjective than objective and requires a knowledge of the inner self as opposed to the exterior environment. That's not to say that investors have to hit a psychiatrist's couch before they stand a chance of succeeding. But knowing your own individual tendencies and inclinations is an important part of the puzzle, and that generally comes from experience and reflection.

My investment hero—Jesse Livermore, that fabulous trader of the 1920s—perhaps said it best. "In actual practice," he surmised, "an investor has to guard against many things, but most of all against himself." That's really not a bad way of putting it. Each of us as a human being is susceptible to the emotional tug and pull of investing, which ranges from complacency in the middle of the market cycle to greed and fear at the extremes. Figure 7-1 pretty well summarizes the range of an investor's psyche that affects all portfolio decisions.

FIGURE 7-1.
THE EMOTIONAL MARKET PENDULUM

The secret, of course, is to be able to recognize where you are on the market pendulum. When you get too *greedy,* you overreach. When you're too *afraid* of the downside, you fail to take advantage of opportunities that seem obvious once the storm has passed. What an investor has to do, as Livermore said, is to guard against himself—to create a psychological environment as devoid of emotion as possible. You need to turn yourself into *Star Trek*'s Mr. Spock and become the Vulcan of the investment world. By doing so, you can kick the extremes of greed and fear out of the investment equation and be better equipped to deal with reality. "Just the facts, ma'am," *Dragnet*'s Jack Webb used to demand, and believe me, that's all you really want when it comes to buying or selling a stock or bond. Eliminate the emotional "you," and you'll have a much better chance of success.

One of the ways to get rid of the "you" is to devise and follow an investment philosophy that is as emotionless as possible. Think of how you might plan an attack on your waistline: you'd have a fairly routinized diet that you'd have to follow; you'd throw away (not hide) all of the tempting high-calorie goodies; you'd announce your goal to family and friends in order to impose a certain outside discipline; and you'd set a target date and weight in order to provide incentive and momentum. In order to succeed, it has to the kind of plan that Mr. Spock would devise and follow. Not necessarily draconian—just Vulcanian: all business, no emotion.

Kicking Out Your Ego

You must approach investing the same way. The best way I've found to do that is to concentrate on the long-term secular view—the same view I wrote about in Chapter 2. By focusing on the secular three-to-five-year outlook, as opposed to the cyclical three-to-five-month forecast, you stand a chance of eliminating the psychological whipsaws that are inherent in money management. The reason is that the long-term primary trend changes less frequently, almost by definition; the short-term direction of the economy or the financial markets is much more susceptible to change. It's the *change* that threatens your emotions. It means that what you thought before might now be incorrect, and your ego is immediately vulnerable; or it means that what you once thought was good now looks bad, and the swing of the pendulum between greed and fear starts to accelerate. At some point, the emotional volatility produced by daily statistics and minute-to-minute price quotes turns you into a brain-dead investor. You've either succumbed to your emotions at the pinnacle of greed or fear, or else you're so exhausted by the process that you conclude, helplessly, that only the pros can do well in this business. Not so. Even the pros are in over their heads unless they have a long-term plan of some kind.

My approach is to start with a three-year-plus outlook for the world and U.S. economy and to work downward from there. It's what we in the investment management business call a "top-down" process. Because you start with the secular outlook, as shown at the top of Figure 7-2, it tends to dominate all other decisions below it.

Try to decide, as I explained in the last few chapters, whether inflation is moving higher or lower, whether the economy will be weak or strong, and what the long-term outlook for corporate profits is. An investor should begin with that Vulcanian road map over the next few years and then adjust accordingly as the business cycle ebbs and flows, making minor adjustments to portfolio mix along the way. By following this plan, you have a much better chance of letting your hard work and intelligence dictate your investment success, instead of letting your emotions get into the way.

FIGURE 7-2.
INVESTMENT DECISION-MAKING PROCESS

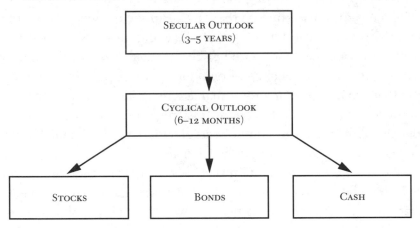

Another way individuals can eliminate the psychological negatives of investing is to place the bulk of their assets in mutual funds. When something isn't directly under their control (in this case, portfolio selection) we tend to worry less about it and kick out much of the emotion. I'll bet, for instance, that you have a *general* idea what price you paid for any mutual fund shares you own but a very *specific* memory of where you bought or sold an individual stock. If you bought IBM at 175, for instance, back in 1987, you know it, and you tell it to your neighbors and friends, along with the prediction that you're going to dump it the minute it gets back to 175, if it ever does. That's emotion talking, not Mr. Spock. Your mutual fund, though?

Well, you think you paid 23 or so and it's "sort of" around that level now; and you think it'll do all right over the long haul because the outlook for stocks over the next few years is attractive. Now, that's more of a "top-down" intellectual argument. Mutual funds help you to move in that direction.

How about routinized methods of investing your cash flow, such as bond ladders, dollar-cost averaging, or simply staying "fully invested" (whatever that means)? In the last resort, I'd have to admit that these formulas are a better solution than thrusting your fragile ego into the midst of that pack of wolves known collectively as "the market" and being whipsawed at the pendulum's top or bottom. You could even utilize some of these plans over a three-year secular time frame and adjust them as your long-term outlook changes. But don't adopt a device that substitutes for sound judgment and intellectual hard work. If it's an ostrich-type "stick-your-head-in-the-sand" proposition, you're not likely to obtain superior results in a Butler Creek investment world.

THE SAVVY INVESTOR:
Bond Ladders and Dollar-Cost Averaging

Bond ladders utilize the technique of buying individual maturities of bonds, which in combination produce a diversified portfolio of short-, intermediate-, and long-term issues. For example, if you were to buy Treasury bonds that mature in 1998, 2000, 2002, 2004, . . . etc., each security would be one step on a ladder of maturities. When the 1998 issue matures, you take those funds and reinvest in a much longer-dated Treasury bond, thus maintaining the ladder going forward.

Dollar-cost averaging, on the other hand, involves the rather simple technique of investing the same dollar amount of money on a periodic basis. For example, you might invest $500 from your salary every month. If bond or stock prices are higher than they were during the previous purchase period, you buy fewer shares. If prices are lower, you are able to buy more shares with the same amount of money, thus "dollar-cost averaging" as time went along. Statistics show that an investor who practices dollar-cost averaging will, in the long run, enjoy a lower average cost per share than the average price of the same security, over the same time period.

If You Have to Play the Game, Use an Alarm Clock

If these "top-down," "mutual fund," "dollar-cost averaging" ideas strike you as too boring, too mundane, and not nearly exciting enough to generate the returns you're seeking, my last bit of advice is to turn inward and shake hands with your ego. If you can't kick the "you" out of investing, make sure you know who that "you" is and how he or she reacts to varying circumstances. If you get emotional at bull market peaks or bear market bottoms, write yourself a note and stick it on the wall in your den, kitchen, or office, enjoining yourself to act, during critical times, like Mr. Spock instead of the average investor.

Better yet, make yourself an investment alarm clock. Let me explain. Perhaps the best way to work your own psychological tendencies to practical benefit in the markets is to determine when your investment alarm clock goes off and act accordingly. Almost all investors have an investment alarm clock that wakes them up, gets them out of bed, and stimulates investment decisions. Each of our clocks, however, is set at a different time.

FIGURE 7-3.
THE INVESTMENT ALARM CLOCK

Now, if you were to randomly set your alarm clock without knowing what your daily schedule was or even when you usually go to bed, a reasonable hour might be 6:00 A.M. Six o'clock might be a little early or a little late, but it would probably let you get the kids up in time for school or get to the office by 8:30 A.M., maybe even both. Let's say, then, that 6:00 A.M. is the perfect time to wake up, and let's say it's the right time in terms of buying or selling stocks and bonds as well. In other words, if your investment alarm clock always rang at 6:00 A.M., you'd be pretty close to the top of the market if you were selling and pretty close to the bottom if you were buying.

The problem is that because of emotion and the associated fear and greed that all investors harbor within their little capitalistic brains, our alarm clocks don't usually go off at 6:00 A.M. A lot of investors, for instance, will sell not at the market top but at the very bottom, when fear finally flushes them out of the market. That's what creates market bottoms, of course. In alarm-clock terms, though, you've just woken up at 9:00 or 10:00 A.M. You've sold way too late to be successful—the smart money has already been up and at 'em and sold as the markets were beginning to go down.

Some might wonder whether this habit of "sleeping in" is really a reflection of the lack of information that many individual investors suffer from. Perhaps, but today's world of investment information on TV, radio, and the Internet makes it easier than ever to stay current. Even with all the information at one's fingertips, there will still be a tendency on the part of many investors—including professionals—to deny its significance. Emotion frequently overcomes logic.

Other investors, instead of being too late, will either buy or sell too early. Their alarm clock goes off at 3:00 A.M., and although you could claim that they're still going to make money, I would suggest that those three hours of missing sleep will take their toll as they try to wind their way through the investment world later in the day.

Every investor has an alarm clock that goes off at around the same time every day. The secret is to know when and to adjust accordingly. If yours goes off at 10:00 A.M. and you really need to get up at 6:00 A.M., buy a brand-new alarm clock that goes off four hours earlier. If yours goes off at 3:00 A.M., turn the darn thing off or hit the snooze button eighteen times, until it's probably 6:00 A.M. *Then* pull your investment trigger. Guard against yourself, as Livermore would say, by rigging a new series of alarms to wake yourself up closer to that optimal 6:00 A.M.

I've been personally working on this for the last twenty years with some degree of success, although I suspect I'll never get it completely right. My investment alarm clock usually goes off at about 4:30 A.M.—not all that early, really, but early enough to do some damage if the bull or bear market is especially volatile. By knowing that's when it goes off, I've learned to push that snooze button at least a few times before I buy or sell. In so doing, *some* but not all of the emotion is kicked out of the process and the facts—"just the facts, ma'am"—are allowed to dominate.

Above all, remember that investing can be a psychological art. The safest approach is to reduce the ego, focusing on the top-down secular outlook, but when the ego enters the picture, it helps to recognize your own personal tendencies and to adjust your alarm clock to wake you at the right time every investment day.

EIGHT

How Not to Get Scalped

Diversification and Fee Management

As the saying goes, "You don't know what you've got till it's gone," and I can swear to that in spades, or in this case—in blades. Hair has always been a particularly sensitive topic with me—probably because there was a long time when I never had any, then a stretch when I had a lot, then a time when I didn't, then . . . well, perhaps I should let the story speak for itself. There's fun in the telling and maybe a lesson or two for all those who care about their hair as much as I treasure mine.

The fact is, I never really had any hair until I was eighteen. I grew up with a flattop treated with lots of butch wax—the skinniest kid with the shortest hair in the 1950s. Scissors were never the tool of choice for my barber; the blades just couldn't get that low, and the only option my parents ever gave me was to ask if I wanted to leave a little "sideburn"—a question I must confess I never did understand until I was in college and in charge of my own hairdo for the first time. What a joy it was to have hair, and lots of it! The Beatles were invading the States, and I was intent on being the first on campus to out-Ringo Ringo. (Or maybe it was Paul. No, Ringo; I was never that good-looking.) I can remember standing in front of the mirror late in my freshman year and declaring myself a "hair god." It was long, thick, and ready for girls to run their fingers through, if only I could get up the courage to ask one out on a date.

Then fate stepped in. Early on a Saturday morning while driving to pick up doughnuts for that day's fraternity rush, I skidded on a downhill snow-covered road, plowed head-on into an oncoming car, and went sideways into my windshield on the passenger side. You never feel a thing, they say, and it's true, but I was bleeding profusely, and as I staggered into the emergency room of Duke Hospital, which just happened to be two blocks down the road, the look on the nurse's face told me I was in deep trouble. "Let's have a look," the doctor said calmly as they stretched me out on the gurney. But then he lost all composure and issued what has to be the all-time classic bedside-manner blunder. "Son," he whispered gravely, "there's not a thing I can do for you."

Oddly, although I probably didn't have much blood left, I didn't *feel* as though I was dying. What had he noticed that had led him to such a grim conclusion? "You see," he said, "you've lost the top of your head. You've been scalped, and I have nothing to sew back on. If someone could go back to the accident and get the scalp—" He stopped in midsentence. Feeling like General George Custer, I had just about resigned myself to joining the hair fairy in the sky when in walked a blessed highway patrolman holding my scalp by the tips of his fingers. "Does anybody need this?" he asked. (God's truth—I was not hallucinating.)

"That's *just* what I need!" the doctor exclaimed, and the rest is history, or should I say *hair*story. After two plastic surgeries, my golden locks grew back, but only in time to have them shaved off again as I crashed into a Hell of another sort—Navy boot camp. Three years in the service kept it short, then it got long again, and now—well, as any fifty-two-year-old man knows, you fight to hold on to every blade you've got. You'll pardon me, though, for being extrasensitive about my hair. Dead men tell no tales, and not many scalped ones do either, but I'm living proof it can be done. Just don't be asking me when I'm going to get a haircut. The subject still makes me nervous.

Lessons from Las Vegas

My scalping was one of the seminal events of my life. The operations that followed made me vow to stay out of the hospital for as long as possible thereafter, and I've been a fitness aficionado ever since. The time I spent in the hospital also allowed me to while away the hours learning a recently devised system for playing blackjack. It was that experience, as you'll soon find out, that eventually led to my career in the bond market. Of course, I'm not recommending a scalping for any of my readers—either in or out of the market—but my scalping ultimately led to my career, and for that, at least in retrospect, I'm more than grateful.

After leaving the hospital and graduating from Duke University in June 1966, my goal was to win some money playing blackjack. I was about to become one of Las Vegas's first card-counting blackjack players, following the initial efforts of a real pro and the originator of blackjack theory, Ed Thorpe. I had no clue that my four months at the tables in Vegas were to lay the foundation for a successful career on Wall Street. But what I learned there taught me several important principles that I've employed for the past twenty-five years at PIMCO, and I figure if they've worked for me, they can work for you, too.

Professional blackjack utilizes a system of counting cards. If you know what cards are left in the deck, you can determine whether the odds are in your favor or lean toward the house. Most of the time, of course, the casino is favored, but there are instances when the deck favors the player and it's at those times that making large bets will tilt the overall long-term odds toward the player. Knowing when to strike with a big bet, however, is no guarantee of success, because even when the odds favor the player, they still only *lean* in his direction. If you accept that reality, it would be foolish to shove all of your money out onto the table for any one play of the cards. Fifty-two percent of the time you might double your money, but 48 percent of the time you'll be wiped out. That's the type of gambling casinos thrive on because it typifies poor money management.

No, when the odds are in your favor, your bet has to be large, but not so big that it jeopardizes your bankroll or your nest egg, as the case may be. The theory is formally labeled "gambler's ruin" but it might well be called "portfolio diversification." Long before Harry Markowitz at UCLA dreamed up the theory of diversified risk that eventually won him a Nobel Prize in economics, blackjack players were onto the same principle: you must not bet all your chips at one time, because if you're wrong, the results will be disastrous.

Think what this implies when it's applied in the investment arena. Obviously, it means that you don't want to own just one stock, just one bond, or even just one piece of real estate (unless it's your home and that's all you can afford). Your investment portfolio should consist of an appropriate mix of stocks, bonds, and perhaps real estate. Despite what many investors currently think, stocks do not always move in an upward line. The recent annualized stock market returns of 15 to 20 percent cannot continue forever, because our economy and corporate profits simply can't grow that steadily that fast. There are also traumatic periods of time—long relegated to the history books—called recessions, that produce sharp, sudden downturns in equity prices. If all you own is stocks, you'd better have a very long-term horizon and the psychological ability to withstand lots of short-term or even medium-term pain when the next recession inevitably comes.

Portfolio diversification, then, is a fundamental principle of investing that should be influenced by one's age, financial condition, and willingness to assume risk.

Portfolio Diversification and the Big Bet

That's pretty basic stuff. I've found, though, that the second half of the story is just as important. When the odds favor the player, it's incumbent to make a *bigger* bet. If you don't do it during the few times the cards favor you, the house will inevitably win. In investment terms, that means that when you have a really good idea, one that you're confident of and have done your homework on, you have to step up and make a large—though not potentially disastrous—bet.

Do you really like a particular stock? Put 10 percent or so of your portfolio on it. Make that idea count. Are you confident that emerging market debt is attractive for 1998? Same thing. Good ideas should not be diversified away into meaningless oblivion. If you've got fifty stocks in your portfolio, you've got too many. If you've got ten mutual funds, you're too diversified. Concentrate, but don't put all your money into any one thing. That's gambler's (or investor's) ruin (see Figure 8-1). On the other hand, don't diversify yourself so much that you're left with portfolio mush. You won't beat the pack that way. As a matter of fact, you're sure to resemble it.

FIGURE 8-1.
DIVERSIFICATION

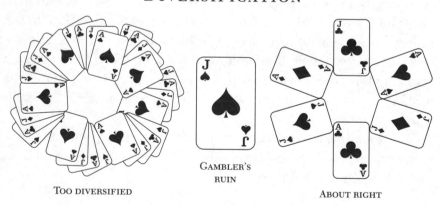

TOO DIVERSIFIED
GAMBLER'S RUIN
ABOUT RIGHT

To get a little more specific, let me suggest that an investment portfolio valued at $50,000 or less should almost invariably be invested in several mutual funds only. There's not enough money there to diversify effectively with individual stocks and bonds, and the brokerage fees alone would wind up costing you a significant percentage of your capital. At $50,000-plus, you should still have those mutual funds, but you can begin to purchase individual stocks that have been properly researched and are appropriate *long-term* holdings. Bonds are still too hard to buy in small quantities for any investor with less than $500,000 in his or her portfolio. With less than that, stick to mutual funds unless you're going to buy the new inflation-adjusted Treasury bonds (discussed in Chapter 13). Those should be easier to obtain and will offer excellent long-term performance.

Keeping Fees Low

When I was playing in Vegas that summer of '66, usually for sixteen hours a day, I was always astounded at how players on a hot streak would tip the dealer large amounts of money. Don't get me wrong, I know dealers have to make a living, too, and I've done my share of tipping as well, but I did it when I left the table and in moderate amounts. Those who were throwing money at the dealer when they were winning were virtually eliminating their chance of coming out on top. They were enjoying the game, I suppose, and were very popular, but in the end their paychecks were left on the strip and not in their wallets.

I realized later that the same theory applies in investing. In this case, the "tips" take the form of commissions on individual trades or expense fees on mutual funds. Think about it. When the investment table is overflowing with profits, it's the easiest thing in the world to pay above-average commissions or management fees. With stocks up 35 percent or so in 1995, for instance, why should you begrudge your mutual fund manager a 1 percent tip or fee? Why should you worry about a full-service commission on a trade that made you $5,000? There's enough for everybody!

The problem is, in the long run, there's not. When you get on a losing streak or your returns moderate into single-digit territory, that 1 percent management fee becomes a heavy load. And that, dear reader, is exactly where Butler Creek is taking us. The average U.S. stock fund charges a fee of 1.35 percent on assets under management annually, while taxable bond funds levy nearly 1.0 percent (according to *Morningstar Mutual Funds*, a Chicago newsletter). In a world of 6 percent, you can't afford to pay a 1 percent bond management fee, nor can you pay it for stocks that might return 7 to 8 percent per year. In the era of 6 percent, that 1 percent fee is more than 15% of your annual income. Stretched out into the long-term future, that suggests that you're turning over 15 percent of your wealth to money managers or brokers. As the Beatles used to sing—"Noooo, you can't do that." When you sell your house, for instance, you pay a realtor's commission of only 6 percent. Why should you pay 15 percent for much more liquid stocks and bonds?

The key is to keep your "tips" and your expenses low in a Butler Creek world of 6 percent returns. Shop as intensively for low fees as you do for excellent money management or top-notch investment research, and if you find them all in one package, hold on to it for dear life.

THE SAVVY INVESTOR:

Investment Research

I believe you've made a good move in your investment education by buying this book, but you'll need updates as well as expert opinions about changing trends in the investment markets. Here are two ideas.

For information about the best money managers, look to the Morningstar or Value Line mutual fund rating services, instead of the magazine article at the newsstand that describes the hot guru who's been able to return 35 percent over the past twelve months. These services look at funds and their managers over one-, three-, and five-year time frames and interview the managers frequently as well. I know—I'm on the phone a lot with the services. You'll benefit from their research.

For updates, here is an offer you may not be able to refuse. I publish a once-a-month *Investment Outlook* that is similar in style and format to most of these chapters. (They even have the personal vignettes that some of you may enjoy.) I'll be glad to offer you a one-year subscription to the *Outlook* just for writing and letting me know how you liked this book. Address it to me at: PIMCO, 840 Newport Center Drive, Suite 360, Newport Beach, CA 92660.

The fact is that the annual cost of owning mutual funds and having money professionally managed via separate institutional accounts has been rising steadily for more than a decade. This trend has gone largely unnoticed by small investors and is just beginning to attract the attention of institutional fiduciaries. This is so even though the assets under management have soared by 3,200 percent in the past fifteen years. Typically, with such enormous gains in "productivity," you'd expect price *decreases,* as in the computer industry, but no such luck here. My industry, like the legal profession, refuses to acknowledge the competitive nature of today's world and continues to charge exorbitant fees for very little, if any, value added. Funds use a multitude of excuses to justify higher fees: higher expenses and the need to satisfy so-called star managers are frequently used rationales. But most of the explanations are nonsense. This year alone, investors will pay nearly $20 billion in annual fees to stock and bond funds, and that figure doesn't include sales charges as well as fees on separately managed institutional accounts.

TABLE 8-1.
How Much You Should Pay

	Average Fund Fee	Ideal Annual Fee	Maximum Acceptable Fee
Foreign stock funds	1.45%	.50–.60%	.75%
Domestic stock funds	1.35%	.35–.50	.65
Corporate, mortgage, and government bond funds	.97%	.25–.45	.50
High-yield bond funds	1.23%	.35–.50	.60

The fees shown in Table 8-1 are what I believe to be acceptable and maximum fees that you can afford to pay in a Butler Creek world of 6 percent. To check on yours, refer to *The Wall Street Journal*, which every Monday lists every mutual fund's expense ratio in the mutual funds quotation section of the paper. Take a look at yours, and if they're above my maximum, think seriously about a replacement. There are hundreds upon hundreds of mutual funds listed in the *Journal* that have annual fees of 1 percent–plus. Some are even in the 2 and 3 percent bracket. These funds will have to display some pretty heady performance to justify that expense, and you'll be bucking a head wind all the way. Instead, you might take a look at the funds offered by my own firm, PIMCO, or, if you prefer a different product, look for those under the Vanguard section, a mutual fund complex headed up by the legendary John Bogle.

Betting Against the House

Whichever investment manager or fund family you choose, it's important to recognize another important point that I observed in the city of neon lights. Very few players left Las Vegas with their wallet or purse intact. After all, the reason Vegas is there in the midst of that sprawling desert is because it's financed by its gambling-crazed visitors. The losers may claim that they were "entertained" and their money was well spent, but the end result was and will forevermore remain the same—the house almost always wins.

It's generally the same story in the financial markets. With the exception of a few rare funds, experience has shown that it's very hard to beat the house—in this case, the market itself. The reason is that individuals and professional money managers, via mutual funds and institutional accounts, generate billions of dollars in commissions as they frenetically move securities to and fro. Even if you accept the premise that "we are the market," two plus two does not equal four, because you have to deduct Wall Street commissions, plus of course those mutual fund fees and expenses, from the results. After doing all that, the equation is not $50 + 50 = 100$, but $50 + 48 = 98$, or a reasonable approximation thereof.

It's Wall Street's job, of course, to convince you otherwise. They're in the business of selling stardust, and people have always been willing to reach for the stars when it comes to making money. The problem is that most investors wind up in dusty Las Vegas instead of Heaven, giving up a substantial part of their grubstake to the house for the supposed comfort of professional fund management. Money managers will seek to convince you otherwise. If they've got a poor long-term track record, they'll tout their most recent twelve months. If they've had a bad year, they'll talk about how they took less risk. I can't count the number of equity fund managers who have told me that the reason they underperformed the market in any particular historical period was that their clients didn't want them to take a lot of risk. They're very satisfied with 12 to 13 percent in a 15 percent market, they'll claim. The money keeps coming in, they argue, and *that,* after all, is the proof of their value. Baloney. Professional money management, with a few exceptions, is a gigantic rip-off, because the product is not worth the fees you're asked to pay.

Fund managers, though, set up countless props to make it appear to their audience that their magic is genuine. A fund family, for instance, will introduce a host of different portfolios with different styles and degrees of risk. Some invest aggressively using leverage and more volatile stocks, while others play the defensive side with lots of cash and low-volatility holdings. If the market booms, they'll tout the former. If it sinks, they'll talk up the latter. It's all stardust that's really sand, I'm afraid.

Another device is to split the market into small and large cap stocks, technology and cyclical stocks, or growth and value stocks, in an attempt to confuse and obfuscate. "Sure, my value-oriented port-folio underperformed," they'll admit, "but that's because growth stocks were hot. Just wait until next year." That's unfortunately what most investors do. They wait and wait, but next year, like Godot, never comes.

Instead, investors fork over billions of dollars annually to pay money managers to play little games. Not only that, but these "pro-fessionals" go home at night comfortable in the feeling that they're a benefit to society and worth every penny! Don't get me wrong; I think there is a need for professional money management. Without it, you might lose a lot more than 1 or 2 percent of your grubstake annually. But unless a manager can beat the market over a long pe-riod of time, he or she has no business being paid superstar fees.

What's an investor to do? My solution is relatively simple. Find the few managers with better-than-market track records who charge low fees. To assist you, subscribe to Morningstar or Value Line, two sources that rate mutual fund performance and report on managers' annual fees. If you can't afford to do that, check out the funds at your local library. If any of that sounds overwhelming, the best alternative is simply to buy an index fund and stay even with the market instead of giving up 1 to 2 percent a year. PIMCO's index fund called "StocksPLUS" not only mimics the stock market but has added 1 percent a year to the performance of the S&P 500 by actively man-aging short-term commercial paper that serves as collateral for S&P futures contracts. If that's not your cup of tea, try Vanguard's Index 500. Over the long run, you won't do much better than these two standouts, and, as I've pointed out, you're likely to do much worse.

Betting on the Long-term Outlook

The last and perhaps most important thing I learned in Las Vegas was to focus on the long-term outlook. Seems like a strange lesson to learn in the city of instant gratification, where all it takes to make you smile is a quick payoff at the tables or your favorite slot machine. Still, when I left Las Vegas in October 1966 to become—I hoped—a Navy pilot, I knew there were things I could have done better, and focusing on the long term was one of them. I'd made money, sure— in fact, I'd turned $200 into $10,000 by working seven days a week, sixteen hours a day (a little more than $5 an hour, by my rough calculation—barely more than today's minimum wage!). But I'd wasted a lot of that time moving from table to table, waiting for a "lucky" dealer, or just sitting and sulking if I'd lost money in the past few hours. What I'd known but hadn't put into practice was that the more time my money was at work—the longer it was in play—the more I would have made. I was so preoccupied with the immediate and the short term that I failed to take advantage of longer-term probabilities that were invariably in my favor as I counted cards.

I never forgot that lesson, though. During my first few years as a portfolio manager in the early 1970s, I made that mistake the cornerstone of my investment management philosophy. *Invest with a view toward the long term.* Don't let short-term market movements or aberrations deter you from looking at the world with a three- to five-year secular telescope. Forget the short-term nonsense. So what if the newspaper says that housing starts were up strongly in July, meaning interest rates have to go up? So what if a TV business reporter tells you the semiconductor industry's book-to-bill ratio moved lower in August and that high-tech stocks were hard hit? I don't think you should ignore that information. But these are just pieces of a gigantic puzzle—a puzzle you have to put together and think about from a conceptual point of view, one that depicts the long-term picture of the world's economy and financial markets. You may not have time to put this puzzle together by yourself, in which case you should choose your asset classes and mutual funds according to the Butler Creek scenario outlined in this book. If you do have the time, though, make sure that the pieces fit together in some coherent, long-term view that encompasses at least three years. If you don't, you're playing into the hands of the casino and you're sure to get fleeced—or, better yet, scalped. That smarts—as General Custer and yours truly can certainly attest to.

NINE

Selling the Noise

Understanding and Coping with Volatility

"A merry Christmas, Uncle! God save you!", cried a cheerful voice. "Bah!", said Scrooge. "Humbug! . . . Out upon merry Christmas! What's Christmastime to you but a time for paying bills without money." "Christmas is a good time," replied his nephew, "a kind, forgiving, charitable time . . ."
— Charles Dickens, *A Christmas Carol*

"Give to the neediest," read an item on the fifth page of *The New York Times* this December past. It was there as a filler and to promote the *Times*'s annual charity drive, but also, I'm sure, as a heartfelt sentiment during the holiday season. The more I thought about it, though, the more it troubled me—not from a sense of guilt but because of my usual philosophical perplexity of not having hard answers to serious moral and practical questions. Give what? And to whom? The longer I pondered, the less sure I was of the answers.

Who are "the neediest"? Well, the homeless, of course; the Somalis; those with AIDS; the abused; abandoned children. Good God, Bill, the answer is right in front of your face. Only a Scrooge could deny that these are the neediest and that what they require is a combination of care, love, and shelter to make a difference in their lives. Down with Scrooge! Up with people!

But maybe it's just not that easy. For instance, in a world of limited resources, if you had to choose one or the other, would you pick gift "A" or gift "B":

A Food for all the starving people of the world for one year
B Farming equipment, irrigation systems, and the professional know-how to grow more food in the future

Many would choose "A" out of a combination of compassion and the logic that says you can't help people very much if they're already dead. Indubitably correct. But what about "B"? Are we as "givers" just going to hop from crisis to crisis, from Bangladesh to Ethiopia to Somalia to wherever, putting out fires but forgetting about fire prevention? "B" should get some votes, too.

Let's explore the question further. Pretend you're a trustee of a foundation with the funds to support only one humanitarian project. Two people have applied for your help. The first contestant is Mother Teresa, who has devoted her life to the needy, toiled endlessly for the sick and hungry in India, and served as a role model of altruism and compassion throughout the world. The second is a goofy, introverted scientist working for Grains Are Us by the name of George McScrooge. No one likes him, he never relates to people very well, but he has a driving passion to develop a drought-resistant strain of wheat that will feed the world, and he's on the verge of producing it.

Who gets your vote? Mother Teresa saves the living. McScrooge may save the yet-to-be-born. Each gives a different set of gifts to a different set of people. I don't know the answer. All I know is that we choose our roads in this world and then walk down them, and to some outside observers it seems that they lead to nowhere, but to others they lead to a city on a shining hill. Maybe in the end they all lead to the same place. Maybe Mother Teresa, McScrooge, and everyone in between who ever gave anything from the heart will all find their special eternity together. I wish I knew, but I'm afraid only

God does. As for us mere mortals, "giving to the neediest" is no simple matter.

Learning to Live with the Bomb

Having to choose between the present and the future reminds me of the dilemma investment managers have when they're assessing bond and stock market volatility. Current techniques of measuring volatility assume that the future will resemble the current market environment, but that's not necessarily so. Markets can be volatile or not so volatile, and the value of many investments hinges directly on the outcome. Those who focus exclusively on the present may be neglecting future benefits that will reap even greater rewards. This chapter will show you how to capture future yields due to professional traders' miscalculation.

Whenever anyone wants to stress just how volatile markets have been, all they have to do is bring up October 1987, the granddaddy of all financial roller coasters. I remember that day, and though I'm a bond manager and wasn't responsible for any stocks, it was still incredibly exciting. The previous Friday, the stock market had closed down 100 points or so in the last hour, so there was lots of anticipation as I woke up Monday morning at 5:00 A.M. (The stock market opens at 6:30 A.M. out here in California. You've got to be bright-eyed if not bushy-tailed real quick, or you'll miss the entire trading day!) I got to work early on this particular day, but in retrospect I'm not sure what for. My professional partners and I simply sat in front of our screens, mesmerized by the fall. Here I was, witnessing one of the most dramatic crashes in market history, and I was sitting on my hands. For someone who takes a long-term secular view, perhaps that might seem appropriate, but the crash had definite longer-term implications for bonds: if 500 points taken off the Dow meant a substantially weaker economy, bonds would probably benefit. Still, I did nothing all day—the plummeting Dow hypnotized me, and I missed the chance to make millions of dollars in the subsequent bond rally.

I confess, I *hate* volatility. It makes me do the wrong things at the wrong time. Volatile markets make me wake up in the middle of the night wondering what's going to happen the next morning. When something does, I usually do the wrong thing. There's little doubt, too, that volatility in the bond market in the past decade or so has been higher than that in the 1960s and '70s. Figure 9-1, provided by Ed Hyman at ISI Group, shows that. However, at least in the past few years, volatility has had fairly tight interest rate bounds—6 to 8 percent for almost all of the past five years. The reasons for this narrow range have much to do with the germination of the Butler Creek scenario, as well as the fact that the economy itself has been much less volatile than in the 1960s and '70s, as seen in Figure 9-2.

FIGURE 9-1.
30-YEAR U.S. TREASURY BOND YIELD, 1960–1996 (MONTH-TO-MONTH % CHANGE)

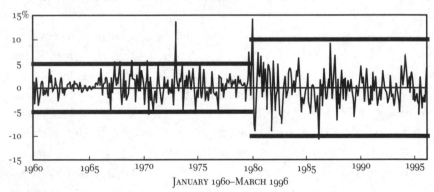

JANUARY 1960–MARCH 1996

Source: ISI Group.

The volatility we've seen in the past few years, which has caused conservative investors to wonder whether bonds are appropriate investments, has been due, then, not to economic conditions but to bondholders' creating their own nightmare. There's not a commentator or guest expert on TV who'll claim that the market's not going to be volatile in the future. Their forecasts are generally on the mark, but that's because of the vigilantes, not the economic fundamentals.

FIGURE 9-2.
REAL U.S. GDP, 1960–1996 (QUARTER-TO-
QUARTER % ANNUAL RETURN)

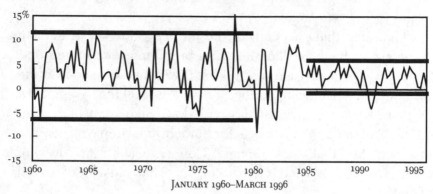

JANUARY 1960–MARCH 1996

Source: ISI Group.

The placid Butler Creek scenario does not claim that volatility has disappeared. It *does* suggest that future volatility will have tight economic bounds and that long-term Treasury bond yields will be in the range of 5 to 7 percent until the year 2000. That's a different kind of world than other money managers are gearing up for, and it appears to create an opportunity that I'll explore later in this chapter.

Selling the Noise

While downplaying the fundamental forces that create volatility, I must still acknowledge that volatility plays a huge role in bond market strategy. Anytime you buy a bond, you're either *buying* or *selling* volatility. With embedded options attached to almost every bond in the marketplace, choosing the proper position on market volatility is critical. Most corporate bonds, for instance, have call options attached. A thirty-year corporate bond can usually be called or refunded by the issuer within five to ten years; in effect, this means that the corporation has the option to pay you back if *it* wants to. In this case, in effect, you've sold an option, that is, sold volatility to the issuer. If interest rates drop a lot—if the market is volatile—you're going to lose your high-interest-rate debt by having it called away from you.

The same thing happens in the mortgage market as individual homeowners by the millions exercise or fail to exercise their option to prepay their mortgage and replace it with one with a lower interest rate. The effective maturities, or what we call the "average lives" of mortgages, go streaking up and down like a cheetah after a gazelle, based on the prospects for homeowner prepayments. It was this volatility that took Orange County, California (my home county), to its knees and into bankruptcy. That and a lot of leverage, of course.

THE SAVVY INVESTOR:
How Options Work

An option gives the buyer the right, but not the obligation, to purchase or sell a security at a certain price within a specified period of time. That's a mouthful, isn't it? It took me several months of business school to figure it out completely. The important fact is that when you buy an option, your potential loss is limited to the premium you pay. At the opposite end of the spectrum, when you sell an option, your potential loss is much greater and in some cases open-ended.

That would seem to shift the advantage to the buyer, not the seller, of options. The buyer of an option is really purchasing something resembling a lottery ticket: the buyer can lose only $2, but the jackpot might be in the millions. But, do you really think the lottery is going to lose money? If the price of the ticket is high enough (and, as you'll see in this chapter, I think it is), then over time, lottery ticket sellers—and option sellers—will be the real winners.

You may wonder what bondholders or mortgage buyers get in return if they are selling or granting all these options and volatility every time they *buy* a bond. The benefit comes in the form of a higher yield. Callable corporate bonds yield ½ percent, or 50 basis points, more than noncallable debt, on average. And GNMA mortgages, which are guaranteed by the government, yield more than 1 percent, or 100 basis points, more than U.S. Treasuries of comparable maturity. That's what I mean when I refer to selling volatility. You "sell" it for a higher yield on your bonds. In the case of these callable corporates or mortgage pass-throughs, what you're selling is really a call option. You allow the issuer to call or take away your security at just the wrong time. Other issues, though, have implicit puts attached to them and force you to buy more securities at an artificially high price.

The question, of course, is how much extra yield is enough, given certain volatility assumptions. That's where the computer jockeys come in with their millions of calculations, trying to figure out just what is fair and what isn't. The average Joe or Jane can't do that, of course, but there are one or two big points to keep in mind. The first is that most bond managers, while correct in their incorporation of volatility measure for valuing bonds, make the mistake of *overestimating* the degree of volatility. In doing so, they invariably overemphasize the value of government bonds versus nongovernment issues in their portfolios and purchase issues that are overvalued on the yield curve, which they believe are worth their lower yields in volatile market environments. Let me explain.

Investment managers can use any number of past time periods to measure volatility, but the most common range is between ten and ninety days. Options and bonds with optionable characteristics carry a value that projects into the future the same volatility that has recently been experienced. To give a simple example, if the Dow Jones Industrial Average dropped 200 points over the past month, stock options would likely be priced on the expectation that the Dow Jones would vary 200 points, up or down, over a similar time period in the future.

This assumption, however, is false. Investment managers and many academicians operate under the assumption that volatility is random, one aspect of the so-called efficient market hypothesis. In fact, major price movements have fundamental economic and political bounds. If interest rates on long-term Treasury bonds were to skyrocket from 9 percent to 10 percent over the next three months, classic option theory would suggest that long-term bonds would likely exhibit the same price volatility in the ensuing period (up or down) and should move within a range of 10 to 11 percent or 10 to 9 percent. The fatal rub for this theory, however, is that the 10 percent yield, in and of itself, is enough to slow economic growth and force interest rates back down. The 11 percent scenario, then, while just as probable as 9 percent under strict option theory, becomes fundamentally and indeed politically less likely than its downside counterpart.

Option volatility, therefore, becomes overpriced because its extreme upside and downside "legs" or "trees" are *not* random and are therefore likely to be truncated. If the 11 percent scenario is less likely because of economic bounds, upside volatility has a lower probability. Mathematical models, however, do not account for this because it is a *subjective*, not a mathematical, judgment.

An even more compelling argument comes from the co-originator of the original option-pricing model devised in the mid-1970s, the late Fischer Black. Black coined the term "noise," which he applied both to the financial markets and to financial market volatility. Noise, Black said, is to be contrasted with information. Those who buy stocks or bonds on information are akin to, let's say, Warren Buffett, the value-oriented stock investor whose long-term

THE SAVVY INVESTOR:

The Efficient Market Hypothesis

Over the past several decades, as academia has exerted its influence on Wall Street, a theory known as the "efficient market hypothesis" has been thrust into the limelight. In brief, it states that at any point in time, stock and bond market prices fully reflect the knowledge and expectations of all investors. If you believe in this theory, you would consider it futile to seek undervalued stocks or to forecast forward trends in financial markets because likely future events have already been factored into the market, and any new piece of information will immediately be reflected in a change in prices.

There's a certain amount of logic to this theory, particularly in today's heavily wired, information-laden markets, but it fails to take into consideration investors' psychology. Markets invariably move to undervalued and overvalued extremes because human nature always falls victim to greed and/or fear. In addition, many investors today make decisions based upon "momentum," which assumes that what happened today will continue to happen tomorrow. This is hardly an "efficient" use of information, and it provides the basis for considering stocks and bonds cheap or expensive based on fundamental considerations.

record of success is legendary. Those who buy stocks or bonds on noise are typified by traders in the futures pits, who buy and sell constantly, based often on rumors, perceived trends, and news that may or may not be relevant. Traders' perceptions are injected into the markets in the form of intensified trading and wider price movements than would normally occur without them. Some of the price movement may have nothing to do with fundamental information at all but may simply reflect the game playing of traders in the pits as they seek to outmaneuver their competition. Thus the term "noise."

Now, Black contends that noise destroys market efficiency. In effect, it creates inefficient markets that move even in the absence of new information. But this makes it possible for astute portfolio managers to add value to their clients' portfolios. In a 1986 *Journal of Finance* article, Black limits his discussion of noise to the mispricing of low- versus high-priced stocks, but he opens the door to the mispricing of options as well. "Because of market noise . . . the short-term volatility of price will be greater than the short-term volatility of value," he writes. If so, then money managers who use short-term volatility estimates for longer-term option valuation are systematically overvaluing option prices. The prices of the options should be lower because the noise is a valueless appendage. This distinction between short- and longer-term valuation is critical, because most of the optionable characteristics of bonds (corporate calls, mortgage prepayments, and selected futures contracts) are longer term in nature but appear to be priced on ten- to ninety-day volatility histories.

How can investors take advantage of this mispricing? Value, as Black would call it, can be bought or sold, depending on its price. According to the above discussion, however, it seems a legitimate objective to gear our strategy toward "selling the noise." Noise, over the long term, is relatively worthless, and selling it makes all the sense in the world. Volatility can be bought if the conditions are right, but noise should always be sold. To me, all else being equal, that implies a bias toward mortgage pass-throughs, and in some instances corporate bonds, though the latter have so many options that it's often difficult to discern what is value and what is noise. Each of these sectors contains options that the buyer is effectively selling to the issuer. If these options are range-bound by economic fundamentals and if their valuation includes noise that fails to take this into account, the purchase of mortgages and callable corporate bonds will benefit in a Butler Creek world.

In a sense, this strategy is the reverse of the "portfolio insurance" that gained notoriety during the October 1987 crash. Portfolio insurers sought to minimize portfolio fluctuations by buying put and call options on the stock market itself. The theory was appropriate until the market became so volatile that they couldn't move quickly enough. Noise or traders' panic had destroyed their methodology. Portfolio insurers bought the noise. We have, for a number of years, been selling it.

If you expect to do well in the bond and financial markets of the late 1990s, you should understand this principle of selling the noise. In effect, you want to concentrate on yield and not on price movement when it comes to fixed-income securities, because noise will exaggerate their yields to the upside. That doesn't necessarily mean loading up on junk bonds, but it does mean buying lots of callable corporate bonds and mortgage pass-throughs, as I alluded to above. In the slow-growth, 6 percent total return world of Butler Creek, there's little fear of high prepayments on mortgages or sudden refundings on corporates.

TEN

Echoes from Africa

Derivatives and the Nature of Risk

If I sang a song about Africa
of the spotted giraffe, the hyena's laugh
of the fiery sun rising to meet the day
with a stillness belying the lion's evening meal;
would Africa sing a song about me?

If I remember a time once in Africa,
bride at my shoulder, chasing a leopard's shadow
with human eyes and Nikon shutters wide apart
Invading the solitude of blackened ancestors;
would Africa remember a time once with me?

If I knew a story of Africa
capturing a disappearing continent for a moment in time
Fleeting—for briefer than the earth's reign;
At least until its dusty death,
would Africa know a story of me?
                    —With appreciation to Isak Dinesen
            and my wife, Sue, for this poem's inspiration

I once traveled to Africa, as you might have guessed from my poem, and it's been a part of me ever since. Being perhaps the cradle of civilization if not of life itself, Africa casts an eerie glow over the entire history, and indeed meaning, of existence. There's a strange beauty to it—this eat-or-be-eaten land—brutal, yet just, even loving, beneath its violent surface. I think it's how I view my own life. I saw *myself* in Africa, and through my own eyes I saw you there too.

Humanity's struggle is much like the one that takes place on the Masi Mara plain of Kenya; more "civilized," of course, and with a higher list of priorities once the main meal is over and done; but the day-to-day battle goes on in much the same way it did centuries ago. I often wonder if we've progressed much as a species—whether civilization is a function more of oil, electricity, and computer chips than of our evolution to a higher order of animal. If our delicate web of commerce were to suddenly break down, would society's behavior become "every family for itself" and then "every man for himself"? I believe it might. When a lion's stomach is full, he can be as passive as a twentieth-century house cat; when it's empty, he becomes a killer. The only difference between "us" and "them" may be that we've figured out a way of keeping the refrigerator stocked. All of our egocentric definitions of the human race—based on our ability to love, feel, laugh, smile, and pray—may be as shallow and mercurial as the twenty-four hours from one meal to the next. That's why I saw you there in Africa—right next to me.

Will Africa remember me? This is another way of asking whether anything we do on this Earth has a lasting impact or whether our actions are as ephemeral as life itself. One of the ways in which we do differ from animals is that we know we will die one day. This consciousness elevates us to a higher level of animal, while retaining the "eat-or-be-eaten" characteristics of the lion. Because of this consciousness, we hope we'll live on through our children and our good deeds. We'd like to think we've made a difference. But will anyone or anything at the end of our lives be better for our time on Earth? I know nothing of any grand scheme of existence, but I wish there to be one, if only to give meaning to our precious moments of happiness and periodic hours of despair.

Bond Mutants

One of my first jobs at Pacific Mutual Life Insurance Company in 1971 was to supervise the clipping of bond coupons in our gigantic vault located in the basement of a downtown Los Angeles office building. We didn't actually use scissors, as the term "clipping" connotes, but we did physically rip coupons off the bonds, much as you would with a book of postage stamps. The coupons were then sent by mail to the issuers of the bonds for timely payment of interest. Those were like the last few days of the Pony Express a hundred years before: old-fashioned, outdated, and on the doorstep of a revolution. Over the next twenty-five years, bond management evolved from the passive clipping of coupons to the hyperactive trading and daily turnover of financial futures contracts on the floor of the Chicago Board of Trade. Compare an image of a clerk with a green eyeshade accumulating bond coupons in 1971 with that of a six-foot-four-inch trader screaming buy and sell orders at the CBT in 1996, and you'll understand what I mean by a revolution.

For the most part, these dramatic changes, which have encompassed new financial instruments and technological innovations to facilitate trading, have been positive additions to the investment environment. Indeed, the swing toward globalized commerce, the reduction of trade barriers, and the rapid economic progress of emerging nations may be substantially a result of this financial marketplace evolution/revolution. Economic growth and finance are inextricably linked; one cannot survive without the other. But recently, investors, regulators, and government authorities of all shapes and sizes have come down hard on an amorphous group of financial market instruments called "derivatives." Some people speak of derivatives the way we once spoke about the bubonic plague—stay as far away as possible! Clients have fired investment managers for owning them, even when they made lots of money.

What are these things called derivatives, and why are they suddenly on everyone's "out" list? A derivative is a financial instrument that either mimics the performance of a bond or is in fact a piece of the bond itself. Financial futures, for instance, which have been around since the late 1970s, are considered derivatives because they are contracts that call for the delivery of bonds upon expiration but are not bonds in and of themselves. Bond options have similar characteristics, as do what are known as interest rate swaps, where the income from one bond (usually one with a fixed coupon whose rate never changes) is swapped for the interest payment from another (usually one with a floating-rate coupon whose coupon varies based on changes in short-term interest rates). In addition, there are what are known as CMOs, or collateralized mortgage obligations, in which a pool of ordinary mortgage loans has been sliced and diced into a bunch of different pieces in order to more narrowly define the maturity or average life of the mortgage itself.

THE SAVVY INVESTOR:
Mortgage Derivatives

Most derivatives are created by breaking up a security and selling off the pieces. Mortgage derivatives are produced in the same way. An investment bank accumulates a large pool of mortgages—say, 1,000 home loans from various parts of the country. It then breaks the 1,000 loans into numerical categories that reflect the monthly principal and interest payments (plus potential repayments) of the entire pool. For example, the first twenty-four monthly payments might be segregated into one derivative called a CMO, or collateralized mortgage obligation. If an investor were to purchase this CMO, he or she would have a very-short-term piece of paper with a fairly well-defined maturity. The later payments, however, say those for months 268 to 280, wouldn't be as definitive. If an investor were to buy this strip, many of the 1,000 mortgages in the pool might be prepaid before month 268 comes around. In that case, an investor banking on a longer maturity would be sorely disappointed, and the value of the CMO would be reduced.

Almost all these vehicles, if used properly, allow their owners to hedge or manage their exposure to the risks of interest rate changes. Some of them can *reduce* risk while *lowering* return, while others can *increase* risk with the possibility of producing *higher* returns. None of them is inherently evil. Derivatives are akin to atomic energy: beneficial if controlled and disposed of properly, destructive in unsophisticated hands. For instance, if the manager of a bond or stock fund wants to reduce its exposure to the market, he can do so quickly and at a relatively low cost by selling financial futures instead of less liquid bonds or stocks. Managers can also buy the market itself in a matter of minutes by purchasing stock index–related futures and then take their time accumulating specific issues when offered at appropriate prices. Similarly, holders of mortgage loans who may have been hurt by the tremendous fluctuation of monthly prepayments but still want to earn a portion of the higher yields associated with mortgages in general, can buy a CMO with a narrow band of potential average maturities and avoid most of the negatives associated with prepayments.

The Risks of Derivatives

It's not the benefits of derivatives, however, that have captured the headlines. Instead, they have become famous for their role in the bankruptcy of my own local government, the now-infamous Orange County, California. The risks are what the skeptics and regulators perhaps appropriately zero in on, and the risks must be analyzed in order to decide whether or not these vehicles are worth the advertised return. What are the risks? There are several.

Credit risk is the risk that a counterparty to a contract will fail to make a payment as required. With derivatives, there is usually a trustee, securities firm, bank, or clearinghouse that is responsible for channeling interest or margin from one party to another. If a financial futures contract goes up, for instance, the "long" (the one who owns the contract) gets what is known as daily maintenance margin, and the "short" has to pay it. A clearinghouse or middleman is responsible for collecting funds from the loser and disbursing it to the winner so that all accounts are clear and settled at the end of every day. As long as the clearinghouse is regulated and financially solvent, such activity is a tremendous asset for the users of financial futures contracts. It prevents the accumulation of IOUs and ensures that all of the participants will be whole.

It is important, however, to analyze the creditworthiness of each intermediary and, of course, the legality of the contract that enforces the obligations of each party. Some banks and securities firms that serve as intermediaries can load up their balance sheets with not necessarily hidden, but certainly hard to evaluate, obligations that could ultimately jeopardize the value of the derivative itself—whether it's an interest rate swap, an option, or any other form of financial derivative. To require an individual to perform an intensive credit analysis is more than a stretch, it's close to impossible. Individuals should, therefore, confine their derivative investments to those traded on government-regulated exchanges, namely financial futures and options. Institutions, though, if they're to survive in this brave new financial marketplace, had better do their homework and do it daily. If not, a future financial accident might be lurking just around the bend.

THE SAVVY INVESTOR:
Types of Risk

Investors tend to think of risk as the possibility of losing their money, but another type of risk occurs when investors *fail* to do something and thereby miss out on an opportunity for gain. Fear of the former kind of risk often leads investors to be more conservative than they actually should; fear of the latter often encourages aggressive investors to overextend by taking chances they ordinarily wouldn't for fear of missing the boat.

In addition to these two general descriptions of risk, there are specific areas of risk that investors should be familiar with:

1. *Operating and financial risk:* Companies with substantial operating risk or operating leverage (high fixed costs such as interest expense and rent) are vulnerable during economic downturns. Financial risk associated with financial leverage refers to the amount of debt a company has on its balance sheet: the more, the riskier.

2. *Interest rate risk:* Bonds and even stocks are vulnerable to the ups and downs of interest rates. Though the issuer of your bond may be of the highest quality, the value of that bond can (and did in 1981, for instance) drop to as low as 30 cents on the dollar because of accelerating interest rates.

3. *Liquidity risk:* Even though a company may be thriving, if there is no established market for its shares, a shareowner may suffer a substantial discount if he has to sell quickly. That's why there's safety in numbers, at least when it comes to providing entries and exits for nervous investors.

Aside from the credit risk, the major problem of derivatives is that they can change character very quickly. You know the story of Humpty-Dumpty, don't you? First, he was a solid, upstanding egg—a pillar of his kingdom, in fact. But once he fell off that wall, none of the king's horses or men could save him.

In the past few years, a Humpty-Dumpty scenario has led to financial ruin for Orange County and other institutions. The entire

HUMPTY – THE CASH BOND

HUMPTY – THE DERIVATIVE

egg is equivalent to the underlying asset on which a derivative is based—a bond or mortgage that goes up or down in price depending on whether interest rates are falling or rising. The derivative is like a piece of egg, purchased for its special characteristics by a particular investor. Some of the pieces, though, are hard to recognize, and it takes a sophisticated computer to know what their prices are going to do under varying economic scenarios.

Mortgage derivatives such as IOs (interest only strips), POs (principal only strips), inverse floaters, and (last and certainly least) kitchen sink bonds (you guessed it—they contain all the garbage that's left over) can become long-term bonds or short-term notes with only slight variations in yields. When a concentrated portion of any of these is scrambled together, leveraged, and cooked over a hot-interest-rate fire, you've got potential disaster à la Orange County.

In the final analysis, though, the problem lies with the chef and not the derivatives: either the portfolio manager didn't know how to cook an omelette in the first place, or he was distracted and failed to pay attention to the temperature of the fire. The derivatives were just pieces of the original egg.

Where does this leave the investor who trusts his or her cooking to someone else, or even one who wants to put the chef's cap on his own head? The individual investor had better order hard-boiled eggs only—sticking to exchange-regulated futures and options as well as plain-vanilla mortgage bonds offered by GNMA and other government agencies. Fiduciaries in charge of corporate pension and 401(k) monies, though, must exercise their supervisory skills to ensure that the mutual funds or investment managers they select to manage client funds have the computer systems and sophisticated personnel to monitor changes in their derivatives' average maturity and duration. If not, they could be in for lots of surprises. Scores of clients and their advisers have visited our PIMCO offices in Newport Beach, California—sometimes for several days running—to check on how we keep track of $90 billion every day. If our answers aren't satisfactory, we lose their business. All investors should demand up-front, understandable explanations from their money managers as well, because when it comes to derivatives, Humpty-Dumpty can turn into one giant fried egg instead of the delectable omelette you thought you were about to eat; and if you fail to pay attention to either your investment manager or your portfolio, you may turn yourself into someone else's lunch!

PART FOUR

What to Buy in a 6 Percent World

ELEVEN

Rolling Around Heaven All Day

Basic Investment Strategies for the Era of 6 Percent

"When I get to Heaven,
gonna take off my shoes,
gonna walk all
over God's Heaven."

Summertime is the season when the living is easy. But life inevitably is a four-season affair, and it's the winters that haunt me the most. There's a cold, dark wind in everyone's future, and being prepared for it in no way diminishes the warmth of a July afternoon—in fact, just the reverse.

In observing the final days of family, friends, and sometimes just strangers in a nearby hospital, I think I've begun to understand why some people want to die. First and foremost, of course, is the sheer physical pain, the exhaustion, the constant agony of going on and on. After a while, it simply is not worthwhile to keep on living. Loved ones and friends have passed on, the kids and grandkids have come and departed to live separate lives, and there are fewer people to live for. The plain truth is, at seventy or eighty you've simply been through it all. You don't need another century to experience the pete/repeat of human nature. You've seen it before, and the more you keep on living, the more you'll see it again: over and over, the joy, the pettiness, the betrayals, the renewals; season upon season, breath upon breath; and when the agony comes, it's just not worth it to see a rerun. For that price, you need a grand opening on Broadway, and those just don't come around much as you stumble deeper into old age.

There's another reason, too, I suppose. Some people think they're going on to a better place. I think in this day and age, when religion has waned in Western society, deep down inside most people *hope* rather than *believe* they're going to heaven. Nonetheless, it must make dying a little bit more bearable. Back in the age of faith, religion was so important in daily living that people seemed to have fewer questions about where they were headed. Anne Boleyn, at twenty-nine and facing execution for adultery and "incest" at the command of Henry VIII, asked that her head be struck off as soon as possible. She remarked, in fact, that she drew comfort from the thought that "the executioner is very good, and I have a little neck." On the scaffold she asked the mob to pray for the king, content in the knowledge of her final destination.

Yet if Anne actually got there I wonder whether she was pleased. What was Anne—and the hundreds of millions before and since—so sure of finding in heaven? And why did she think she would be so content up there? Did she just sort of expect to roll around heaven all day, immersed in a perpetual glow, a sort of mental orgasm? Or would she visit with relatives for eternity? The truth is, without a little spice, all the fun things would be impossible. I mean, if you went to a cocktail party in heaven, how could you possibly come home and talk about the other people behind their backs? If you wanted to watch a celestial football game, how could you possibly cheer on the "Heavenly 49ers" versus the "Cowboys in the Clouds"? Both teams would be just sort of rolling around, soaking up the "atmosphere." Quarterback sacks would definitely be out. See what I mean? What did Anne—or what do *you*—actually think you're going to do up there? If you find an agenda or figure out some way to buy a program, please let me know. Given the chance, I'd like to be prepared.

A 2 Percent Inflationary World

While I have little idea of what heaven is like, I have a clear notion of what a heavenly investment portfolio might look like over the next several years. The previous chapters have outlined the expected economic and investment climate for the balance of the twentieth century as well as some tips on how to invest in that type of environment. If you've stuck with me up till now, you know that the economies of the United States, and indeed the world, are likely to be prosperous but noninflationary. After analyzing numerous long-term secular factors, I believe that 2 percent inflation will be the norm for most of the industrialized world. Several phenomena will be chiefly responsible for this near freeze in prices:

1.   A vigorous globalized trading environment will continue to keep a lid on wage growth. Cheap labor in Mexico, China, India, and other major third-world nations will inhibit the ability of industrial nations to raise wages and remain competitive. The tremendous acceleration of corporate downsizing in the United States over the past several years is but one of numerous factors that have prevented labor from gaining even a toehold of leverage in the 1990s. If labor's influence is diminished, only commodity prices remain a threat to the low-inflation scenario, and these should remain well behaved in the tight monetary and fiscal environment I expect.

2.   Central banks and governments must now listen, and listen very closely, to the capital market vigilantes. Stock, bond, and currency investors/speculators have an increased ability to call the shots and even to dictate national policy. If they do not like what they see, money is quickly withdrawn from a nation's economy, and economic chaos is a possible result. We have only to look toward Mexico in 1994 to know what happens when the vigilantes become upset. Although they may not always exert such dominant influence, as long as the vigilantes reign, central bank policy and government fiscal policy must trend toward the conservative. The policies of Gingrich's Congress of the past two years embodied, in part, a response to the

demand by America's voters for less intrusive government, but even more was a reaction to the worldwide stranglehold of the capital market vigilantes. This trend almost ensures that inflation will not accelerate over the next several years.

3. Demographic trends throughout the industrialized world are extremely positive for low rates of inflation. The populations of Japan, Europe, and the United States are aging rapidly, which suggests higher savings rates ahead. More important, the heyday decades of "shop till you drop" will not likely return in this century. "Twenty-somethings," who are the largest relative spenders, are a declining percentage of the population in all G-7 nations. It is no coincidence that retail chains throughout the United States are closing stores and declaring bankruptcy at rates not seen since the Great Depression. With consumption low, inflation has very little chance of rearing its destructive head.

4. U.S. corporate productivity may be in a secular uptrend that will continue for some time. Although part of the explanation is corporate downsizing and the elimination of marginally productive workers, another portion may be due to the accelerating use of computers and other high-technology trends that allow machines and people to work together more efficiently. In addition, the total number of dollars invested by business in plant and equipment (machine tools, production facilities, etc.) has increased rapidly in the last few years, allowing America's productive capacity to grow. That growth reduces the potential for supply bottlenecks and the resulting higher prices that often showed up in the inflationary 1970s. These trends are potentially a powerful anti-inflation tonic.

5. Debt levels are excessively high among government, corporations, and U.S. consumers. Similar conditions exist in other G-7 nations. These high levels of debt make increased rates of consumption extremely difficult and suggest spending growth levels at or below the current annual increases of 3 to 4 percent. This will help keep inflation under control.

The total of all of these trends suggests low inflation and low growth in nominal GDP—an economy that resembles that of the late 1950s and early '6os rather than the late '7os. In case you weren't around then or are too young to remember, Figure 11-1 is a chart of long-term interest rates between 1957 and 1965.

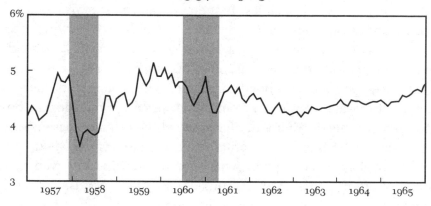

FIGURE 11-1.
PRIME LONG CORPORATE BOND YIELD,
1957–1965

Source: Salomon Brothers, Inc.

Pretty low and not very volatile, wouldn't you say? That's a Butler Creek environment. While interest rates back in 1958 got as low as 4 percent, we should not expect such a miracle this time around. There's too much demand for capital worldwide, and there remains a group of savvy investors who have seen skyrocketing inflation in the 1970s and '80s. Trust only goes so far, you know, and if yields ever stayed in the 4 percent zone for long, there might be lines of willing sellers ready to take their profits, including yours truly! But a range of 5 to 7 percent is certainly reasonable. And if that's the case, total returns on bonds over the next several years will average 6 percent. The important corollary to this 6 percent forecast for bonds is that stocks aren't going to do much better. Typically, they've returned about 3 percent more than bonds in these moderate-growth environments, so we're looking at less than double digits for equities as well.

Income Versus Price

What can an investor do in such a "boring" economic and investment environment? How does one eat and digest what I once labeled "slow-growth soup"? Before getting into the specifics, I should explain some broader principles. Remember, an investment's *total* return comes from a combination of income and price performance. In the case of bonds, it is interest and price; for stocks, it is dividends and price. During dynamic *bull* markets, such as the one we have had since 1982 for both bonds and stocks, a substantial portion of total bottom-line return has come from price appreciation as opposed to income distribution. That's one of the primary reasons why individuals who buy bond mutual funds on the basis of yield, and yield only, have done so poorly when compared with those who view markets from a total-return approach. In other words, investors seeking to maximize their interest income may succeed in the short run, but in the long term, their total return has been limited because their bonds have shown less price appreciation. Take a look at Figure 11-2 to see what I mean.

FIGURE 11-2.
ANNUAL TOTAL RETURN, 1982–1995

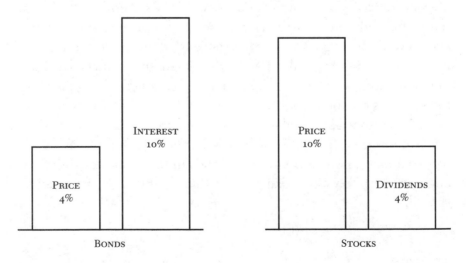

Thus, in dynamic bull and bear markets, successful bond and stock managers have focused more on price than on income. For bonds, even though interest constitutes a larger portion of the total return than price, the latter has clearly separated the women from the girls. Looking at stocks, the difference in favor of price is beyond dispute. For markets that meander instead of skyrocket, however—Butler Creek markets that move back and forth in a relatively narrow range—a different theoretical and philosophical approach is required because the price movement of bonds will be limited. Instead of focusing on price, an investor should do a U-turn and begin to focus on yield. Instead of looking for capital gains, an investor should strive to maximize income (see Figure 11-3).

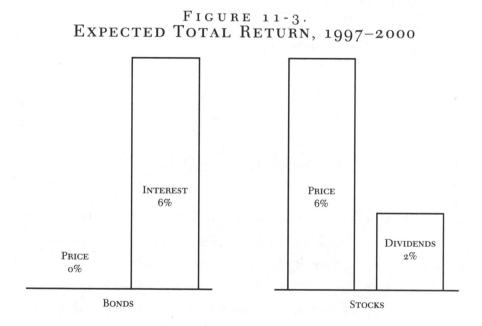

FIGURE 11-3.
EXPECTED TOTAL RETURN, 1997–2000

This approach, of course, has its limitations when applied to the stock market. I'm not about to recommend shifting entire portfolios into, for example, utility stocks that produce high dividend income or into the highest yielders in the S&P 500. There will always be a place for growth stories, especially, as we'll see, in the international arena. In addition, for individual investors, the tax advantage afforded by capital gains from price increases is still sizable and should be take advantage of.

But on the bond side, the picture changes markedly. High income will be the winning strategy for the balance of the 1990s, and learning how to get it will be the key. Notice I said "high income," not "high yield." These days the term "high yield" is associated with junk bonds, which are rated Ba and lower by the bond-rating services, and clearly most bond portfolios should not focus exclusively on junk bonds. While a small portion of your portfolio might well benefit from some attractive junk bonds, the thrust of your strategy should be to maximize income from bonds in higher-quality categories, government debt, A- and Baa-rated corporate debt, and mortgage pass-throughs.

THE SAVVY INVESTOR:
High-Yield Bonds

"High-yield" is the 1990s term for what used to be known as "junk" bonds. It seems that when these bonds perform well, they take on an uptown nickname, but when they go down, they're just called junk. Technically, any bond that carries a quality rating issued by Moody's or Standard & Poor's of BB or lower is a high-yield bond. Any bond with a rating of BBB and higher is called "investment-grade."

I think investors can benefit by owning a well-run high-yield fund, but with two qualifications. First, stick to funds that purchase bonds at the top of the "high-yield" rating scale. Many issues rated B or C may be close to bankruptcy, and their risk is closer to that of a penny stock than a U.S. Treasury bond. So stick to BBs if you can. Second, realize that because of their lower quality, junk bonds tend to mimic the price behavior of the stock market in the short term. When the economy and stocks do poorly, high-yield bond prices suffer in comparison to those of high-quality U.S. Treasuries. Holders with a long-term perspective, however, should do well with junk in comparison to government bonds, since their yields tend to average 3 to 4 percent higher per year than Treasuries' do.

How to Reach for Income

In a high-quality world, how does one go about increasing one's yield and income without running a higher risk? Well, reaching for yield is rarely done without additional risk. The only virtually riskless asset is a short-term Treasury bill. Everything else is subject to market volatility, and prices will fluctuate according to interest rate- and credit-related trends. So an increase in risk over and above that of T-bills is ensured no matter what you do. The secret is to find the strategy with the least amount of risk and the greatest increase in return, though some investors will emphasize avoiding risk while others will strive for increasing return.

In a Butler Creek environment, where interest rates move in a mild, low-volatility range of 5 to 7 percent, the risk of bond ownership itself is significantly reduced. If long Treasury yields climb to no higher than 7 percent, you're way ahead of investors in the 1960s and '70s, who came to call bonds "certificates of confiscation": as interest rates skyrocketed to the high teens, bond prices sank lower and lower and it seemed as if investors' capital was eroding so fast that it was being confiscated. Your chance of losing money over the next few years, however, will be sharply reduced. Investors, then, can increase the maturity of their investments over and above that which they might otherwise consider to be prudent.

My investment strategy therefore, is:

Lengthen the Maturity of Your Bond Portfolio

This doesn't necessarily mean building a portfolio of 100 percent thirty-year Treasury bonds. It does suggest, however, that money market funds and short-term securities will not be attractive alternatives during the rest of the twentieth century. But a good intermediate-term bond fund, or a portfolio of five- to seven-year notes should be an attractive holding. In fact, with what we bond managers label "rolling down the yield curve," intermediate-term maturities approaching seven years should come close to or even exceed the yield of long-term thirty-year Treasury bonds over the next several years.

My second strategic recommendation is:

Invest in Foreign Markets

Our global economy is chock-full of attractive investments, both in bonds and in stocks. To confine your portfolio to the borders of the United States would be folly. Europe has some extremely attractive, high-quality opportunities on the bond side, and the emerging markets offer debt partially backed by the U.S. government that's yielding between 11 and 15 percent. Your equity portfolio will also benefit from the higher-than-average growth rates of Asian and certain South American economies.

Third on the list of critical strategies is:

Stress Yield at the Expense of Prepayment Risk with Your Bonds

Corporate bonds and mortgage pass-throughs are subject to what is known as prepayment risk. Almost all the debt issued in these two giant arenas is subject to retirement, at the *issuer's* option, prior to maturity. While this is negative for bondholders, as an inducement they are offered higher yields, ranging from .25 percent to 1.5 percent extra annually. While such bonds were sucker's bets during the bull market of the past fifteen years (because they were invariably called or retired before maturity), when the tables are reversed in the less volatile market of the future, grabbing the yield will pay handsome rewards.

My fourth strategy that shows considerable potential is:

Purchase Some U.S. Inflation-Indexed Bonds

These bonds are supposed to be issued for the first time in early 1997. They offer individuals the potential to beat inflation by 3 percent or more for the duration of their maturity. Very few bond investments have been able to do this over the past fifty years, so these instruments may serve as a good investment in the Butler Creek scenario as well as a good hedge if I'm wrong and inflation takes off.

The last of my recommended strategies is:

Remember That Stocks Don't Always Outperform Bonds

Although stocks are definitely the best bet for the long haul, there have been periods as recently as the early 1970s when bonds and even money market funds did better over a ten-year time frame. It would be a mistake to structure your personal portfolio with 100 percent stocks, especially considering the income advantage offered by bonds in a Butler Creek environment. (Administrators of institutional funds should likewise remember this admonition when deciding whether to retain the standard 60–40 stock bond mix for retirement funds.)

All these strategies deserve further amplification, which the next few chapters will provide. Above all, remember that in a Butler Creek world the techniques of both bond and stock investors that were successful in past decades will have to change. Here's to the future—and to total returns that may not be as heavenly as in past years but will let you sleep at night as though floating on a cloud.

TWELVE

Men Behaving Badly

How to Ride the Yield Curve in the Era of 6 Percent

Women: You can't live with 'em and you can't live without 'em. We guys have known that ever since we popped our first pimple, and all along we've sort of assumed that the ladies felt the same way about us. Now, I'm not so sure—the part about not being able to live without us, that is. Biologically, it seems men are just a sperm bank away from extinction. Morally, we've been responsible for every war or argument of any kind since Adam told Eve he wished she'd wear her hair down instead of up. And socially—well, if an event or conversation doesn't involve a bouncing ball of some sort or other, we stutter and stammer, check our watches ten times an hour, and finally resort to tugging on our wife's skirt in hopes that she'll say we can go home now. I ask you, ladies—is *that* something you can't live without?

On top of this, almost all of the things that were once exclusively a part of the male's domain are now being done by the opposite sex. Women box, they play football, they even smoke cigars and look good doing it. I walked up to a cigar stand the other day with my wife, seemingly in tow, and the salesman asked, "Can I help you, ma'am?" I'm the same wimp I've always been—the problem is the world won't pretend anymore that I'm still the head of my own household. Macho, macho man is no more. Muncho, muncho man is more like it. Just give us guys some chips and a beer, park us in front of the TV, and call when you *really* need us. You know what I mean by that, don't you, ladies? There's still one thing left that only guys can do and for which there can be *no* substitute: moving furniture. I'd like to see any of you 120-pound, pencil-armed, pasta-fed, salad-munching females move a sofa or a refrigerator. Only a hairy-chested, pot-bellied, red-meat-eating man can do that. So how are you gonna rearrange the furniture or move out on us if there're no guys around to do the heavy lifting? Call up your friends? Consult the "First Wives Club"? Let's see you "steel magnolias" get together and clamp those bony hands on a piano leg or two. Hah! Got you thinkin' now, don't I?

So, I guess it's sort of a draw of sorts. Call it a feminist standoff if you want, but what I now know is that there'll be a valued role for each of the sexes as we move into the twenty-first century, and it won't be much different than it's ever been: women will still control things like they always have, and the men will sit around, drink beer, watch TV, and move furniture once in a while. The more things change, the more they stay the same.

Stretch Those Maturities

Things may not have changed much in the battle of the sexes, but there will be lots of changes in a Butler Creek 6 to 8 percent invest-ment world. As we've seen, under previous financial conditions, you invested with price as your primary bond focus. In the new eco-nomic environment, you shift to an emphasis on income: different strategies under different conditions. The success of this strategy, however, is conditional: if interest rates move outside of my ex-pected 5 to 7 percent range, it can *hurt* rather than heal. With that understanding, let me elaborate on the four strategies outlined in the previous chapter. The first, as you remember, was:

Lengthen the Maturity of Your Bond Portfolio

This strategy, while simplistic on the surface, is actually a very sophisticated move. It's like "castling" in a game of chess—changing the board positions of the king and rook in one step. When it's executed at the right time, it can be quite dynamic and often successful. It's the same with maturity extension. At first blush, a bond professional would likely decide that in an environment where interest rates have fallen about as low as they're going to go, the proper strategy would be to get defensive, *shorten* maturities, and wait for the coming bear market with its skyrocketing interest rates. After all, rates have dropped from 15 percent to 6 percent over the past fifteen years, and the return trip could be devastating. Under a complete reversal, the prices of thirty-year bonds could drop more than 60 percent. Now, that's a "certificate of confiscation"!

But this either/or, black/white strategy is not necessarily the best way to bet. A multiyear stretch of little change and a narrow range of interest rates means that an investor will have to scrape and scrounge in order to exceed the market averages, and the best way to start, I think, is simply to lengthen the average maturity of the bonds you hold.

That notion, of course, comes first from the observation that longer maturities yield more than short-term cash. Figure 12-1 shows two different "yield curves," as we call them in the bond business.

In this chart, the further you move to the right on the horizontal axis, the longer the maturity of a bond. The higher you go on the vertical axis, the higher the bond's yield. The curve itself represents a plot of the various yields associated with various maturities, which change constantly as the market changes. The "normal" curve is one in which yields increase as maturity increases. The "inverted" curve is something different. Sometimes, during periods of central bank tightening, the short maturities yield *more* than the long ones, in which case the curve is said to be inverted. But in a low-inflation environment, with no need for the Fed to "take away the punch bowl," you would have to believe that yield curves will be normal in shape,

FIGURE 12-1.
YIELD CURVES

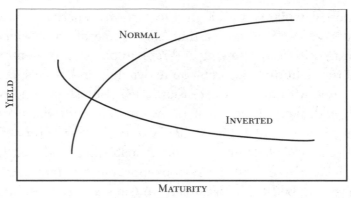

in which case longer maturities will yield more than short-term cash. That extra yield for maturity extension will likely average 1 percent or more when comparing money market yields to five-year Treasury notes. In a low-interest-rate, Butler Creek world, that's a nice piece of change, even considering the additional risk.

THE SAVVY INVESTOR:

Yield Curves Shape

The normal yield curve shown in Figure 12-1 is one in which yields grow as maturities become longer. You probably instinctively perceive this when comparing your money market short-term yields to the long Treasury yields described in the financial press: you get more yield by extending maturity.

Why is this so? There are numerous theoretical

reasons, but one of the most basic is that long maturities carry more risk. With short maturities, you can almost always cash in your investment for 100 cents on the dollar because you risk your money for days, not years. A thirty-year Treasury bond, however, is another matter. Although Uncle Sam guarantees it, your investment is still at risk relative to the ravages of inflation because its coupon, or interest payment, is fixed. Therefore, investors demand a higher yield for thirty-year paper, and the yield curve is higher the longer you extend your maturity.

"Near Cash" to the Rescue

Another valuable insight when it comes to maturity extension is that even when you have to hold cash reserves, it pays to develop cash substitutes, or "near cash," which serves the same purpose but offers higher yields. Other portfolio managers have often marveled at PIMCO's ability to outperform the market year after year. We've done it in almost every twelve-month period for the past twenty years, as a matter of fact. One of the ways we've consistently been able to add value has been our ability to turn short-term commercial paper yields into "near-cash" substitutes with returns 50 to 100 basis points higher. That means buying short-term callable corporates with extremely high coupons—"cushion bonds." It means buying nine- to twelve-month commercial paper with yields 100 basis points, or 1 percent, higher than shorter cash alternatives. It means buying anything whose price behavior will mimic that of one-year maturities or less, but with higher yields.

In our research, which goes back more than twenty years, we

FIGURE 12-2.
NOT GOOD ENOUGH

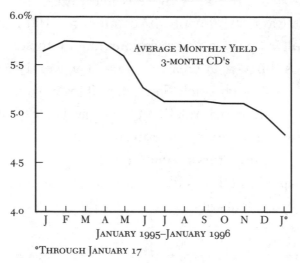

JANUARY 1995–JANUARY 1996

°THROUGH JANUARY 17

Sources: Bank Rate Monitor; The New York Times.

found that an investor sacrifices a lot of yield by concentrating his or her short-term investments in one-month commercial paper or a pure money market fund. That sacrifice is shown in Figure 12-3; it averages about 75 basis points when compared with six- to nine-month maturities. The graph also shows a measure of risk called "standard deviation." That figure, shown on the horizontal axis, is considerable for ten-year notes and even for one- to two-year maturities, but in the six- to nine-month area is only slightly higher than for one-month paper. An investor should always be looking for a pickup in yield with little or no increase in volatility or standard deviation. That's the case here, and it's an ideal situation to take advantage of.

The reason three- to nine-month yields are consistently so much higher than that of one month is the perceived loss of liquidity. There's not much more price risk in a one-year Treasury bill than there is in three-month commercial paper, because both mature at 100 cents on the dollar in a very short period of time. What the pros fear is the lack of liquidity. They want that cash handy in case they find some bargains to invest in during the next few days and weeks.

FIGURE 12-3.
RETURN VERSUS RISK FOR VARIOUS MATURITIES, ONE-MONTH HOLDING PERIODS, JANUARY 1968–DECEMBER 1995 (TOTAL % ANNUALIZED RETURN)

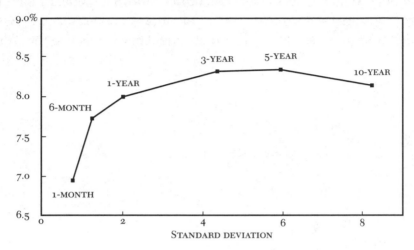

These pros are usually stock market managers who couldn't care less about 50 basis points more in yield on their commercial paper. They're more concerned about the next Internet IPO and making 15 percent–plus a year in annual total returns. For that dream, they pay a big price: they sacrifice 50 to 75 basis points of yield. Extending maturity in the short-term area is the best risk/return trade-off in the business, bar none!

The individual investor needs to use this strategy, too. Almost all individual brokerage accounts have cash reserves, and, of course, millions of investors have money market mutual funds that mimic the one- to three-month commercial paper sector I disparage. What is not so well known is that many mutual fund complexes and brokers offer short-maturity substitutes that invest in paper with one- to two-year maturities. My own PIMCO Low Duration Fund is one of them. Another alternative would be a conservative adjustable-rate mortgage mutual fund. Check out the Morningstar or Value Line mutual fund–rating services for some well-run funds in this area. In a Butler Creek scenario, those funds with slightly longer maturities than, but similar liquidity features as, money market funds should be excellent money market substitutes, offering yield pickups of close to 1 percent.

Remember—in order to compete in the new investment environment, yield and income will be critical. Moving gradually out on the yield curve and stretching your definition of money market securities are two conservative ideas that should pay handsome rewards.

THIRTEEN
That Old-Time Religion

Sleep Tight with Inflation-Indexed Bonds

I am, as I mentioned before, a Father Guido Sarducci Catholic—
which is to say, no Catholic at all. Still, I enjoy attending Mass with
my devout wife and less-than-reverent eight-year-old son, Nick. This
past Sunday, "The Boy," as I affectionately refer to him, had just
come back up the aisle after taking his second Communion and was
rolling the holy wafer back and forth in his mouth like his last Life
Saver at the movies. "Get a whiff of this, Dad," he exhaled, and I
must admit I wasn't sure whether it was the wafer or his earlier-
morning Cheerios I was being asked to experience. Still, I did the
right thing, said it was the body of Christ and that he'd get used to it.
I'm not sure about myself, though.

Although the Communion interests him, Nick's favorite part of
the Mass has always been the doughnuts offered in the parish hall
upon its conclusion. It's all Sue and I can do to keep him from bowl-
ing over the priest as he sprints toward the exit in search of the rec-
tory's chocolate Winchells. Several months ago, he wolfed one down,
got back into line to compliment the Father on his service, and managed to clap his suddenly dark brown palm onto that of Father
Stevens. Ever since then, the volunteers have served glazed doughnuts only, and Nick can't seem to understand why. I think I've fig-

ured out the reason, though, and also why the usher now seats us in the right rear corner of the church. We haven't been excommunicated yet, but we're on the cusp. I've considered instructing Nick to go to confession and say, "Bless me, Father, for I have sinned," followed by the story of the doughnuts, but he's a little too young to understand, and I figure that would be rubbing chocolate on some already sensitive wounds.

I'm always struck by the moment during a Catholic Mass when attendees beseech the Lord to forgive them not only for what they have done wrong but for what they have *failed* to do. Wow! I sometimes think, There's no one in here who's coming out squeaky clean! That, I suppose, is the point—to define the concept of sin so that it humbles you before God no matter what you do—or don't do. But this Catholic concept of sin is so un-1990-ish. It really doesn't square at all with how most of us as modern parents treat our children. Today's focus is not on what our kids did wrong but everything they did right. "Self-esteem," not personal sin, is the critical concept, and we reinforce it a thousand times over before the reality of a cruel world smacks our kids in the face sometime in their mid-twenties— shortly after they've completed their sixth and, one hopes, final year of undergraduate studies. Our kids, we believe, do nothing wrong— they don't even *fail* to do anything wrong, if that mindbender is possible. Smiley faces adorn every piece of work they bring home, even the weekly spelling tests with three errors on them. "Good effort," the teachers coo. My son's hockey team got whipped 9–0 the other day, and the coach heaped praise on them for a good second period when they gave up only one goal. What happened to the old saw, "We'll get 'em next time"?

Our kids are being snuggled, cuddled, and coddled into believing that life is one giant Slurpie at the local 7-Eleven. They'll be adults soon enough, you might respond, and that's true, but the concept of childhood and adolescence as a training ground has been gradually eroded by our emphasis on a child's self-esteem and confidence instead of his or her self-discipline and competence. There's a nice middle ground somewhere, and I think we 1990s parents have lost sight of it. So when it comes to child rearing, give me a healthy dose of that old-time Catholic religion. It's okay for kids to know and acknowledge that they haven't performed well or done the right thing all the time. I'll trade a thousand smiley faces for one of those little wafers anytime. Just give me fair warning, so I can keep my temporary distance from "The Boy."

Bonds with Inflation Protection

If you're befuddled as to where to put your money to work in a Butler Creek environment, Uncle Sam has come up with a potential remedy. It's a remedy that comes as close to resembling an investment with nothing to lose but a lot to gain as anything I've seen in the investment world, and it's sure to put an authentic smiley face on your portfolio for years to come. It's called an "inflation-indexed bond," and, as you will soon be able to tell, I'm *extremely* bullish on it.

In mid-1996, Treasury Secretary Robert Rubin announced that in future years the U.S. government will be in the business of selling inflation-indexed bonds—bonds whose total annual yield is adjusted to track changes in the inflation rate. Inflation-indexed bonds differ from normal Treasury issues in one dramatic way: when you buy a normal Treasury bond, the coupon or annual interest payment is fixed; it won't change from the time you buy it until the day it matures. That's why bonds are called fixed-income investments. The annual payment on inflation-indexed bonds, however, will change based on the changing rate of inflation. If inflation goes up, you get paid more; if inflation goes down, you get paid less.

If your primary concern is earning a stable return that will exceed inflation and allow you to plan for retirement, college education for the kids, or just that extra-special vacation on your twenty-fifth wedding anniversary, these bonds may be for you. They represent a compromise between the roller-coaster, up-and-down, everyday volatility of the stock and bond markets and the staid, low-yielding world of bank CDs and money market accounts. They are close to an outright guarantee that your money will beat inflation, and for that reason alone they're worthy of any investor's consideration, whether that investor is an individual investing $10,000 or my own firm, Pacific Investment Management Company, investing $90 billion.

Although many of the details of these bonds weren't available as this book went to press, the fundamentals behind them are quite simple. Each indexed bond, whether it has a maturity of five, ten, or thirty years, will offer an initial interest rate that should be considered an investor's "real" yield over and above the rate of inflation. For example, let's assume that these new bonds are offered to the market with a stated coupon or interest rate of 4 percent. That might seem paltry, considering you can get 5 percent–plus with Treasury bills and around 7 percent with government bonds, but it's really not. It only seems low because that's the yield *before* the government adds its annual adjustment for inflation. It's what we call the "real" yield, or the yield that would be available if inflation had never existed. We all know, however, that inflation has become an almost permanent part of our lives, so the U.S. Treasury will top that real 4 percent yield off with an annual adjustment for inflation. Let's say inflation in 1997 is 3 percent. Your actual return, or yield, that the government is going to pay you will be 4 percent plus 3 percent for inflation, or 7 percent. That 7 percent looks very attractive when compared to bank CDs, long-term Treasury bonds, or even common stocks. This adjustment process for inflation continues year after year until your bond matures, so if you hold that investment until maturity, you're going to be guaranteed a yield that's 4 percent above inflation no matter what.

ECONOMICS 101
A Brief History of Inflation

Inflation is really a disguised form of tax and therefore has been with us ever since governments have had the power to issue money. In order to get revenues, governments can tax, borrow, or print money, and it's the printing at too fast a rate that ultimately sends prices higher.

Governments tend to print money at especially high rates during wars; thus, you can see in the accompanying chart that inflationary peaks in the United States have been closely correlated with major conflicts ever since the War of 1812.

The formation of our central bank, the Federal Reserve, in 1913 facilitated a generally increasing rate of inflation, because the governors of the Fed can control the growth rate of money and their mandate has been primarily to promote economic growth as opposed to preventing inflation. Prior to that time, the United States was often weakened by severe deflations as the gold supply and agricultural production dominated monetary flows.

U.S. INFLATION/DEFLATION, 1790–1979

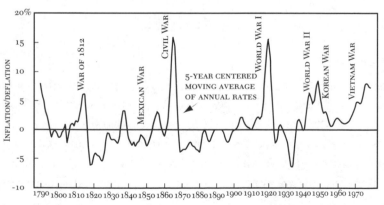

Sources: Securities Research Company; U.S. Department of Labor; U.S. Department of Commerce.

Sounds pretty good, doesn't it? Well, it is. London's *Financial Times* praised the bonds as a "risk-free asset" that "deserve[s] warm welcome." *The Wall Street Journal* wrote that "conservative investors who flock to Treasury bonds for safety may soon have even less reason to worry." I think they're right. But there's a small catch. While you're guaranteed to beat inflation, the price of these bonds will still go up and down on the open market. Not much, mind you, but enough to make these bonds different from Treasury bills or a money market account, in this way: if you must sell the bond before it matures, the price you'll receive will depend on its current market value, which may vary.

The concept of inflation-indexed bonds has actually been used in Canada and the United Kingdom for some years now—Canada since 1991 and the United Kingdom from 1981. Other countries, such as Australia, New Zealand, and Sweden, have used them as well. From their experience, and from exploring the actual mathematics of bond price movements, it's possible to look ahead and surmise to some extent what the volatility of these new U.S. bonds might be. Remember that while you're guaranteed a certain "real" yield over and above inflation, the price of the bond itself may fluctuate. If you decide to get out before the bond matures, you could have a capital gain or a capital loss that could affect your overall return.

Real Yields

Take a look at Figure 13-1, which displays prices of the Canadian inflation-indexed bond since 1991. You can see that the original issue, which was priced at close to 100 in November 1991, has gone as high as 115 and as low as 88 over the last five years. The reason is that even though Canadian investors were compensated at a "real" interest rate of 4¼ percent plus annual inflationary increases, the bond fluctuated in price to reflect an adjustment in what investors demanded from that "real" rate. When it first was issued, the 4¼ per-

FIGURE 13-1.
CANADIAN INFLATION-INDEXED BOND PRICE
CHANGES, NOVEMBER 1991–MAY 1996

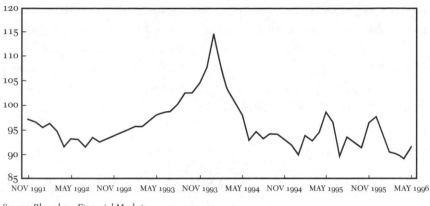

Source: *Bloomberg Financial Markets*

cent real rate looked perfect, and the bond traded at 100. By early 1994, though, investors thought that 4¼ percent was higher than what it should be, so they drove the price up and the real yield down. Later on, they thought 4¼ percent "real" wasn't enough, and the bond's price sank to 89 in order to raise the "real" yield to something closer to 5 percent.

My point isn't to confuse you but simply to suggest that U.S. inflation-indexed bonds are going to move up and down in price based on investor expectations, as well as supply and demand. So be prepared for price fluctuations and either a profit or a loss if you don't hold these bonds until they mature.

Hypothetical Performance Comparisons

Despite this relatively minor negative, these bonds should have a place in almost any investor's portfolio. Because they will allow purchasers to know with certainty that their investment will beat inflation if held to maturity, holders will be able to rest somewhat easier at night without wondering if their existing funds will be adequate to beat the ravages of future inflation. Although their current nest egg may not be enough to maintain their existing lifestyle after retirement, they will know that what they do have will be inflation-adjusted and give them a real return of approximately 4 percent. When you compare that to other available choices and their inflation-adjusted returns for the past seventy years, they come out close to the top. Take a look at Table 13-1.

TABLE 13-1.
HISTORICAL INFLATION-ADJUSTED RETURNS*

	1926–1995 Average Return	Average Return After Inflation	1946–1995 Average Return	Average Return After Inflation
Standard & Poor's 500	10.5%	7.4%	11.9%	7.5%
Long-term corporate bonds	5.7	2.6	5.8	1.4
Intermediate-term government bonds	5.3	2.2	5.9	1.5
30-day Treasury bills	3.7	.6	4.8	.4
Inflation	3.1	—	4.4	—

*Returns include price change and income from dividends and interest.
Source: Ibbotson Associates.

If these new inflation-indexed bonds had been in existence over the same time periods and returned an inflation-adjusted 4 percent, only stocks would have outperformed them, and with considerably more volatility. Granted, the Butler Creek scenario suggests that fixed-income bonds will do quite well in the coming disinflationary environment through the year 2000, but what after that? These bonds provide an attractive hedge. Remember, too, that during periods of accelerating inflation such as the 1970s, stocks perform very poorly. While inflation-indexed returns should underperform stocks over the long haul, they may provide a comforting cushion of stability should inflation return.

FOURTEEN

Fifteen Minutes of Fame

Mortgage-Backed Securities for a Great Deal on Yield

There are certain seminal statements that ultimately turn into prophecy. When it comes to the media and our celebrity-ridden modern culture, I can think of three: Marshall McLuhan's "The medium is the message"; Andy Warhol's "Everyone will be famous for fifteen minutes"; and historian Daniel Boorstin's "The celebrity is someone who is well known for his well-knownness." All these oracles recognized the ephemeral nature of fame on a screen as opposed to fame rooted in achievement. The difference lies partially, I suppose, in the durability or longevity of the public's memory, but the media age has progressively blurred the distinction, making an *Oprah Winfrey Show* bisexual transvestite hockey player as famous as a scientist who discovers the gene responsible for colon cancer. Both have their fifteen minutes and then are shoved offstage to make way for the next performer.

This phenomenon of fame is something that has molded my life for a long time now. I'm not famous in the Hollywood sense, but I've had my minutes, and I must confess that fame is something I've always wanted, more than money or power. If I could have chosen one thing when I started down the PIMCO trail in 1971, it would have been to "light up the night like a flame—baby, remember my name." That, I suppose, is a little unusual for the investment business. Most money managers would opt for the lean green, most politicians for power. Perhaps only the artist would choose fame at the expense of the other two. I guess that's what I am at heart—an aspiring artist who happens to be well paid for doing something else.

Over the years, this mix has led to some ludicrous moments: for example, my calling up the business editors of *Time* and *Newsweek* in the early 1970s (at the ripe old age of twenty-eight) to offer my outlook on the markets. Some of them actually picked up the phone. None of them gave me a "print." Then one day a *Wall Street Journal* reporter actually called *me*. Alone in my office on a late afternoon, I was so nervous that I kneeled backward in my chair (my knees on its seat, facing toward the rear), all the while rocking to and fro as I opined on the prospects for bonds. Three minutes into the call, I suddenly pitched too far forward, did a somersault in midair, and landed flat on my back with telephone still in hand. "Anything wrong?" the reporter asked. "Must be the connection," I said and without a pause continued to pontificate from the floor. I didn't realize it then, but at that moment, I literally had nowhere to go but up.

My encounter with fame, to be honest, has been everything I expected. I was tuned in to McLuhan and Warhol early on and realized I could never really "live forever." I did want a bunch of "prints," and I've had more than my share. Still, like the greedy artist I am, I like to con myself into believing I'm only on my seventh minute out of the allotted fifteen. But if it's fame that drives you, when is enough enough? Could a *negative* "print" end my quest for a full quarter hour of celebrity? I don't know. The answer is probably in the last sentence of this chapter, but most of you probably don't much care; you have your own dreams. If they happen to be slanted in the direction of fame, though, be careful. It's a brief candle indeed, and in the end it will leave both of us gasping for oxygen in thin air, no matter how many mountains we've managed to climb.

Those Darned Mortgages

There have been some famous—or perhaps infamous—periods in bond market history involving mortgage-backed securities and the derivatives created from them, but these periods, unfortunately have taken more than fifteen minutes to play out. The tremendous volatility of the past few years, during which interest rates increased from 5¾ percent in December 1993 to 8 percent in late 1994, then reversed course in 1995, has wreaked havoc with mortgages, as prepayments first declined and then increased substantially. This whipsaw movement has been enough to convince investors that mortgages as an investment are not only hard to understand but extremely risky as well.

The perceived risk comes from the potential for almost all individual homeowners to prepay their mortgages in favorable interest rate environments. If interest rates drop and a homeowner refinances, you as a mortgage pass-through holder have just lost a valuable asset; the yield on your portfolio will decline because that higher interest rate disappears. During the past fifteen years' bull market, mortgage loans have not been particularly attractive investments because most have been prepaid and no longer exist. Unlike today's fifteen-year Treasury bonds with original thirty-year maturities, GNMA mortgages with 16 percent coupons that were issued in 1981 have nearly evaporated from the investment horizon; they've almost all been prepaid and refinanced at much lower interest rates. If that 16 percent GNMA was refinanced with an 8 percent mortgage, your income as a bondholder has been cut in half, whereas if you had bought the long-term Treasury bond, you'd still be receiving the high interest rate originally offered back in the early 1980s. Such are the negatives of mortgages in a declining-interest-rate bull market for bonds.

But in a volatile market where interest rates move as dramatically as they have in recent years, investors may be surprised to learn that mortgage-backed bonds, such as those GNMA 16s or even GNMA 6s, do poorly *whether rates are going down or going up*!

Both ways you lose. Sounds impossible, doesn't it? But it's true. The reason mortgages do poorly in bear markets as well as bull is that their theoretical average maturities, based upon expected prepayments, actually get longer because investors no longer expect homeowners to prepay as interest rates rise. This leads to a situation in which a mortgage's maturity is extended at just the wrong time— during a bear market. Of course, just the reverse occurs during bull markets: the higher prepayments reduce the maturity, as I've described above. The net result is that you're stuck with a short maturity during a bull market and a long maturity during a bear market, which is just the opposite of what a bond investor wants. In bond market parlance, your portfolio is said to be "negatively convex."

Over the TOP with GNMAs

Now, the reason I've put you through this complicated analysis is to explain the fact that, since mortgages hurt investors in both up and down interest rate markets, they have to be priced accordingly in order to induce investors to buy them. You don't think an institution such as my own PIMCO would buy something this bad unless it had *some* redeeming qualities, do you?

The redeeming quality of mortgages in comparison to Treasuries and high-quality corporate bonds is that they *yield* more. Because of the negatives of that prepayment option—which almost all mortgages have—they're forced to offer a much higher yield than other bonds of similar quality. These days, for instance, a mortgage loan fully guaranteed by the U.S. Treasury—a GNMA—can be purchased at approximately 8 percent, a yield that is 1½ percent, or 150 basis points, higher than the yield on comparable U.S. Treasuries. Figure 14-1 displays the average yield advantage of mortgage pass-throughs when compared to other bond market alternatives in today's marketplace.

As you can see, mortgages offer more yield than almost any other

FIGURE 14-1.
YIELD ADVANTAGE OF MORTGAGE PASS-
THROUGHS OVER U.S. TREASURIES

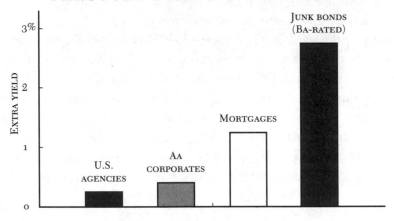

major sector of the U.S. bond market, with the exception of junk and Brady bonds, which are rated less than Baa. For a high-quality-oriented investor, the yield they offer is unbeatable.

But yield, as we've seen, is not the only criterion that makes for a good bond investment. If interest rates are volatile, the average life of a mortgage loan will lengthen and shorten at just the wrong time. However, what if long-term interest rates were going to mimic my old Butler Creek? What if they didn't change much for the rest of the century and meandered lazily along between 5 and 7 percent? Wouldn't mortgage pass-throughs represent about the best value around, especially for those investors who wanted Aaa quality? You bet they would, and they *do*.

Mortgage pass-throughs will represent one of the best-risk/ return investments in the bond market over the next three to five years. Nowhere else will you be able to generate returns approaching 8 percent for government-guaranteed paper in a 2 percent inflationary world. Institutional investors should consider not only overweighting them but allocating as much as 40 to 50 percent of their entire bond portfolios toward the mortgage side. Individual investors who find it difficult to buy bonds in small quantities can easily participate via a host of mortgage-related bond mutual funds.

Check out Morningstar or Value Line for some four- and five-star recommendations. Whatever your avocation, make sure your portfolio is chock-full of mortgages in the coming years—just a plain-vanilla GNMA pass-through will do fine. In a financial world where yield as opposed to price movement is king, you'll want to reach for mortgage loans first and foremost on your list of potential investments. And as for reaching for fame, well, you'll have to make that decision yourself. *My* fifteen minutes, I fear, are almost up.

FIFTEEN

The King of Salamasond

Investing in the Emerging Markets

"I'm Yertle the Turtle! Oh marvelous me!
For I am the ruler of all that I see!"
—Dr. Seuss, *Yertle the Turtle*

You may call me Yertle if you wish. Anyone who's climbed a few molehills is bound to develop a Yertle complex, and I, being human, have succumbed enough times to have earned the title. I whine that my state and federal taxes, for instance, are enough to pay the budgets of several small cities. I observe privately that half the employees at my company owe me their jobs. I mutter that "living well is the best revenge," all the while thinking of past acquaintances who somehow betrayed or didn't believe in me. That's Dr. Seuss material, to be sure.

While balancing on the backs of all my fellow turtles, though, I sometimes do look down, and then I see life from a different perspective. When I do, I realize that instead of my supporting thousands of people, in fact, millions upon millions of people have supported me. All those people at my company, to be sure, but also a heritage of lives in years and centuries past. It's like standing not only on the backs of fellow turtles but on an enormous coral reef of history.

You can go back as far as you want in time to total the accounts payable, but as a Californian I like to start in the 1800s near the Continental Divide. Every time I'm in Wyoming next to the Tetons, or Utah near the Wasatch range, or Colorado at the top of the Rockies, I can't help but wonder "How did they do it?" The settlers of the American West, that is. How did they get over those mountains? What sacrifices must they have endured? It's almost beyond imagination, and something few of us modern couch potatoes could even contemplate doing. Yet they did it, and the result is my home, my community, and the United States as we now know it. Our debt to them is enormous.

If you live back East, you might consider the sacrifices necessary to bring such a simple thing as drinking water to New York City. The lives of hundreds of immigrants, many of them Irish, were lost during the early 1900s in the construction of a maze of aqueducts and underground tunnels beginning upstate and winding their way down to Manhattan. Every time you turn on the tap . . . well, you see what I mean. Millions of lives, forming a reef upon which we thrive. Then, of course, there are the teachers, the doctors, and the scientists who have made modern life possible. I'm alive today because of Sir Alexander Fleming, who discovered penicillin in 1928. When I was dying of scarlet fever in 1946, my doctors decided to use this World War II wonder drug as a last resort, and two weeks later I was playing at home, albeit with a rear end full of more holes than a pincushion. I owe you, Alexander Fleming.

The king of Salamasond was self-anointed. There are no turtle kings, only billions of turtles struggling to survive in their own way and making it possible for their friends and future generations of turtles to have it just a little bit better.

The International Solution

There's lots of rarefied air in the stock market these days and probably millions of Yertles who think that 20 percent annual returns are what life's all about. You shouldn't mistake a bull market for investment genius, though, just as Yertle shouldn't have proclaimed himself turtle king just because he managed to climb to the top of the stack temporarily. The days of double-digit returns are over, as I've explained in previous chapters, and it's time to anoint a new strategy king.

Part of the new strategy involves reaching for higher yield in areas where safety is not substantially sacrificed, as explained in the previous chapter. Another area, though, calls for accepting additional risk in areas that have become attractive bets in today's globalized investment environment. I'm speaking of the emerging markets and the attraction they have for investors who want to inch their total

FIGURE 15-1.
EMERGING MARKET STOCK PERFORMANCE

Source: Datastream.

returns closer to 10 percent, as opposed to 6 or 7 percent. The emerging markets are attractive primarily because their economies are growing faster, which allows earnings to compound at higher rates than in the United States and other industrialized nations. Over long periods of time, equity monies should migrate to where the growth is, and the emerging markets will be the fastest-growing countries of the future, especially in a Butler Creek environment. Figure 15-1 illustrates the past six years of equity returns in Asia versus those of the industrialized world. There's been some volatility, but no comparison really in terms of performance, especially relative to Europe.

E C O N O M I C S   1 0 1
What Are the Emerging Markets?

Before the fall of the Iron Curtain in 1989, certain parts of the globe were referred to as the "third world" or "underdeveloped countries." Today they're described in a much more optimistic tone as "emerging nations" or "emerging market countries." The reason for this shift in emphasis is the acceleration of global trade and the reduction of tariffs and import quotas as our own capitalistic ideology has taken hold nearly everywhere. Instead of being regarded as underdeveloped, these countries are seen as emerging into the dawn of free enterprise. Since almost all of them have at least a rudimentary capital market, we call their stock and bond markets "emerging markets."

You can find emerging markets almost anywhere on the continents of Asia and South America. Eastern

Europe now qualifies as well. Because these countries' economies are still relatively underdeveloped, their growth rates on a longer-term basis tend to exceed that of the United States. Watch out for potholes, though; there are probably more Mexico-style crises in our future.

The cheapest way to invest in emerging market stocks is to buy a "closed-end" fund on the New York Stock Exchange. These funds typically sell at a discount to their actual value. That's right—you can usually buy them at 10 to 15 percent less than what their assets are really worth. My personal holdings of international stocks are almost all invested in closed-end funds. *Barron's* magazine, a financial weekly, lists all the available funds and their discounts to asset value every week.

THE SAVVY INVESTOR:

Open- and Closed-End Mutual Funds

Most individuals invest in what are known as open-end mutual funds. Fidelity Magellan, for instance, is open-ended because it keeps accepting new deposits as well as allowing withdrawals. A closed-end fund, however, accepts only a fixed amount of money at the time of issuance. While its assets can appreciate as much as or more than those of open-end funds, it doesn't allow new contributions.

Closed-end funds are really stocks that trade on an exchange, usually the New York Stock Exchange. To get in or out after the initial offering, you have to buy or sell the shares from or to someone else, as you would any other stock. Because of this characteristic, their price or value often varies from what their underlying assets are really worth. In recent years, investors have been able to buy closed-end funds at a discount to their true worth, a clear advantage to the buyer of closed-end funds.

The Diminished Risk in Emerging Markets

Emerging nation bond markets are also attractive. They provide interest rates of 10 percent–plus and yield at least 4 percent more than alternative investments in the United States, Europe, and Japan. If the *risk* of investment in these stocks and bonds were acceptable, we would obviously have the makings of an attractive long-term strategy. Let's explore that proposition for the next few pages.

The subject of emerging market risk is most appropriately viewed from a long-term secular perspective, the approach I've been recommending throughout this book. The way to start is by diving into your history books and learning that today's emerging markets—such as China, Mexico, Argentina, and Brazil—have been poor investments for much of the past ninety-five years. Many of these countries have defaulted at least once and confiscated private capital in an effort to nationalize assets for the benefit of the "people." Logically, this fact alone should be enough to prevent conservative investors from steering capital in their direction. But with the fall of the Iron Curtain in 1989, a dramatic change took place that promises to appreciably reduce the risk of future default. Let me explain.

The fall of the Iron Curtain meant more than the defeat of communism and the triumph of capitalism; it signaled the accelerated development of a global trading environment, not only by opening up Eastern Europe and Russia as potential trading partners but also by inducing a mind-set among investors and sovereign nations alike of cooperation and mutual dependency. If a nation's prosperity is dependent upon its level of cooperation with and trust from its global neighbors, it becomes much more difficult to walk away from or abrogate contracts. In the 1950s, it meant relatively little to Castro's Cuba, for instance, to renounce its U.S. debt, because Russia appeared to be an attractive alternative source of any funds the United States had previously provided. In 1931, it meant relatively little to Brazil to walk away from its obligations, because exports to the United States and Europe were not a substantial portion of its GNP and a cutoff of future loans or a diminution of future trade with the West was just not that onerous. Thus, the economic consequences were minor.

Now things are different. There's no Communist behemoth to turn to if emerging markets paint themselves into a debt corner, and these countries have become so hooked on the benefits of global trade that the consequences of default would be much more substantial. To renege on one's obligations these days would mean a painfully long period in the financial penalty box while neighboring countries were busily skating around scoring goal after goal, increasing their economic growth and improving their citizens' prosperity.

It's a different environment these days, and the advantage is decidedly in favor of creditors and the capital market vigilantes. For investors, this means that the risk of lending and investing in emerging markets can be an attractive proposition at the right price and with the appropriate timing. Risk has been reduced because of long-term secular changes in the global sociopolitical environment. Potential returns, therefore, now appear more attractive than in previous years.

Another factor to consider when buying or selling on emerging markets is global liquidity cycles, which ebb and flow over several years' time. The late-1994 crisis in Mexico and many South American nations was due to excessive short-term borrowing and rapid political changes, but the fundamental force behind the deterioration of almost all emerging markets for stocks and bonds was the tightening of liquidity by the G-3—the United States, Germany, and Japan. These three major centers of the industrialized world are essentially responsible for the liquidity flow of our modern globalized marketplace. They are the centers of our economic universe. At some distance from this middle zone are the "wanabees" such as France, Spain, and the United Kingdom, followed by the emerging nations on the perimeter (see Figure 15-2).

Nations outside the circle are more or less dependent upon the Big 3 for their life's blood. If U.S., German, and Japanese central

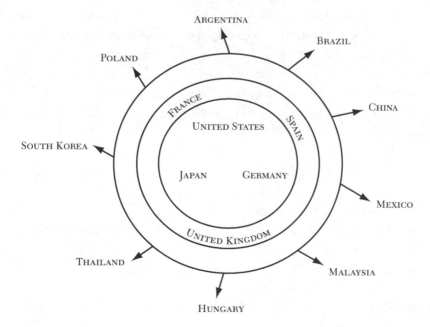

FIGURE 15-2.
CIRCLES OF ECONOMIC INFLUENCE

banks are all pumping out excess liquidity, you can expect the emerging nations to prosper. If the G-3 are reducing liquidity by raising interest rates and tightening the money supply, their dependent neighbors will suffer. The latter set of condition, of course, is exactly what happened in 1993 and 1994. All of the Big 3 were running tight monetary policies with excessively high real interest rates that not only slowed down their own economies but also sucked investable funds out of nations on the periphery. In contrast, when those policies were reversed in 1995 and all three major countries were lowering their interest rates, the emerging market nations began to revive. The lesson is to invest in emerging markets when the Big 3 are lowering interest rates and to pull back when they're raising them. It's a simple rule, but it should be effective in future years. If the Big 3 are not moving together in lockstep, what to do is less clear.

Which Country to Invest In

Now, which countries should you invest in (either stocks or bonds)? Well, it's difficult to point to individual countries, because prices and situations can change rapidly, and by the time this book hits the shelves, specific recommendations could well be out of date. But there are several criteria you should look for when placing funds in *any* country, whether an emerging nation or not, and they are as follows:

1 Excellent prospects for above-average economic growth (4 percent real growth or higher)
2 A stable political environment
3 Low levels of debt as a percentage of GDP (less than 60 percent)
4 A trade surplus, or at least a trade deficit that is *not* consumption-oriented

5   A legal system emphasizing individual and corporate prop-
    erty rights
6   A high savings rate

As I write this, *no* country meets all of these criteria. But many
emerging markets meet five of the six conditions, and it's there the
investor should look first when seeking higher returns in an environment of lower secular risk. According to my analysis, India, Singa-
pore, and Chile are now at the top of the list, although, as I've
mentioned, current prices in those countries may suggest deferring
investment there. Those willing to take slightly more risk would certainly want to consider securities from China, Thailand, Argentina,
and Brazil as well. As mentioned previously in this chapter, stock investors should consider closed-end funds when looking toward
emerging market commitments.

Brady Bonds

On the bond side, individuals can invest in emerging market debt
funds, both open- and closed-end. Wealthier investors with at least
$100,000, and institutions such as my own PIMCO, can invest di-
rectly in a host of debt instruments, many of which are collateralized
by U.S. Treasury bonds. These bonds are called "Brady bonds," having taken their name from former U.S. Treasury Secretary Nicholas
Brady, who, if not the intellectual force behind their creation, was at
least smart enough to give them his blessing. Each country's Brady
bond, shown in Figure 15-3, is a little different from the others', but
the characteristics they share are that the issue's principal at maturity as well as one or two years' interest payments are collateralized
by U.S. Treasuries held in escrow at a major New York bank.

If Mexico had defaulted on its Cetes, Tesobonos, and Brady
bonds back in 1994, debtholders in the first two categories would
theoretically have received nothing, but Brady holders would still

FIGURE 15-3.
THE BRADY BOND MARKET—U.S. DOLLAR SERIES (BASED ON CURRENT AMOUNT OUTSTANDING)

have been able to bank $220 worth of principal and interest out of a $1,000 par value bond that had sold pre-crisis for $630. *In other words, about one third of the Mexican Brady bonds was guaranteed by U.S. government debt.* Table 15-1 shows you the same values for Mexican and other emerging market debt using today's market prices.

This U.S. Treasury collateral is an *important,* though not *exclusive,* justification for buying emerging market debt. After all, these markets are extremely volatile and exhibit price movements more like those of high-beta (high-risk) stocks than fixed-income securities. In addition, as the table implies, approximately three-fifths of the value of these Bradys is dependent on the creditworthiness of the country itself, and for that you have to fall back on an analysis of the country characteristics previously mentioned. None of the countries in Figure 15-3 qualifies in all those areas. Mexico, for in-

TABLE 15-1.
PERCENTAGE OF BRADY BONDS' VALUE
GUARANTEED BY U.S. TREASURY

	Par Value	Market Value (B)	U.S. Treasury Dept Collateral (C)	% "Guarantee" (C/B)	Yield to Maturity
Mexico	$1,000	$680	$230	34%	9.5%
Argentina	1,000	600	200	33	10.2
Brazil	1,000	570	200	35	10.5
Venezuela	1,000	600	220	36	11.5

Source: PIMCO

stance, certainly does not have a stable political regime at this time (late 1996), nor does it have a high savings rate. Nevertheless, with yields in excess of 10 percent, Mexican bonds offer investors a potential way of stretching their overall portfolio return toward the double-digit level by yielding more than the five to six percent offered by U.S. markets. Many of the emerging market bond funds available to individuals have a high percentage of holdings of Brady bonds.

As in other areas, a diversified approach with a limited percentage commitment is the way to invest in emerging market debt. My PIMCO funds, for example, will consider investing up to 5 percent of our total portfolio in these issues, but no more. Individuals who can assume the risk of volatile markets might hold as much as 10 percent. Accidents can still happen, and it's best to sleep well at night in addition to increasing the returns on your portfolio. All you have to do to remind yourself of that is to think of poor Yertle—king of Salamasond no more.

SIXTEEN

Mickey in Wonderland

The Butler Creek Case for Bonds

Sometimes I sit in my den at home and read stories about myself. Kids used to save whole scrapbooks on me. They get tired of 'em and mail 'em to me. They might as well be about Musial or DiMaggio. It's like reading about somebody else.

—Mickey Mantle

Yours truly, the Father Guido Sarducci of Catholics, was back in church on Sunday, contemplating life and trying to keep my eight-year-old son, Nick, as quiet as possible. Sketching on a Saint Catherine's missalette, he created what my wife, Sue, figured was a depiction of Christ's stations of the cross but which he announced was a diagram of a hockey play he was going to employ later that afternoon. He then put me on the spot by asking, "Isn't church boring, Dad?" I ask you, what would any adult male who was missing that morning's 49ers game respond? Should I tell a lie in the presence of the Lord? "Sometimes it is," I finally answered, "but you can learn a lot, too, so stop doodling hockey plays and listen to the priest." Whew! That was one close escape.

So I stopped daydreaming about Jerry Rice and started listening to the homily myself. The priest was stressing the importance of the body and its ascension to Heaven. Roman Catholics believe that the body is an integral part of the human spirit and that *both* must make that trip, just as Christ did. Well, thought I, the eternal skeptic, just *which* body is it that makes the final trip? I hope we don't all go up there as ninety-year-olds with arthritis, wrinkled skin, and incontinence. If there are mirrors in Heaven, I'd much prefer to check myself out as a dashing twenty-eight-year-old with thick hair and a trim waistline. And, Lord, while I'm on the subject of miracles, if I make it, could you revigorate this bladder of mine so that I can get a sound eight hours of heavenly sleep and drink coffee during your business meetings without having to excuse myself every thirty minutes?

Well, one thing led to another, and I got to thinking about how baseball great Mickey Mantle used to speak about his days as a Yankee. In his final years, it seems, he hardly remembered the Mantle who had stroked more than five hundred home runs years before. He wasn't quite sure, or perhaps didn't recall, *who* he had been. It was as if he were standing in front of Lewis Carroll's hookah-smoking caterpillar in *Alice in Wonderland*: "*WHOOO* are *Yooouu*?" demands the caterpillar, and Alice, Mickey, and perhaps all of us are never quite sure. Is our truest self the soul and body of youth in its prime, or are we what we become at the close of life?

This question is a difficult one. At first blush, the correct response is that we are who we turn out to be. Western culture is fond of describing life as a continuum. You start at point A, learn things, gain experience, and finally, at the very end, figure out who you are and what life's all about. But why do we assume that the meaning of life becomes clearest at point Z, instead of M or Q? As Hemingway once wrote, "Old men do not grow wise, they just grow careful." And, of course, they grow senile and suffer from Alzheimer's disease and change in innumerable ways for the worse instead of the better.

"So what?" you ask. Well, I'm back in the pew, still trying to get Nick to simmer down, and I'm thinking about which body of mine I'd like to enjoy up in heaven. But I also have to wonder which mind and soul I'd like to have attached to it as well: the heretical, acidic, vibrant, tempestuous spirit of my youth, or the more mellow, understanding, experienced soul of today? Which was better? Which one was real? Why should one persist and not the other? No one promised this game of life had easy answers. Just hard questions. *Whooo* are *yoooouu*? Who, indeed?

Stocks Forever?

I've got another hard question for you: *Whooo* are these market gurus who want you to invest *all* your money in stocks during the next millennium? Who are these experts who can never conceive of the possibility that bonds might have a place in a diversified portfolio? The gurus, of course, would have a ready response: they would point to Figure 16-1 and suggest that if ever there were a long-term secular argument for anything, this surely is it.

FIGURE 16-1.
REAL RETURNS ON VARIOUS TYPES OF INVESTMENTS, 1801–1994

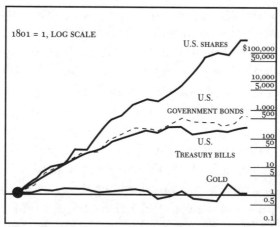

Source: Stocks for the Long Run *by Jeremy J. Siegel.*

This graph, provided by Jeremy Siegel in *Stocks for the Long Run,* convincingly points out that ever since the beginning of the eighteenth century, stocks have hammered U.S. bonds, bills, and gold on an inflation-adjusted basis. Over that period, $1 in stocks would have appreciated to more than $100,000 today, while the holder of Treasury bonds would be left with only $600 or so. In addition to this remarkable difference in asset return, Siegel points out that stocks beat long-term bonds by an average of 3.1 percent a year, and that if you measured the spread in twenty-five-year segments over the entire 195 years, bonds beat stocks on only twenty-six occasions, or in 15 percent of the periods. All those periods, by the way, occurred before the beginning of the present century.

Now, I'm a guy who went to Las Vegas and made a tidy sum of money by playing blackjack and betting large sums of money whenever the odds were in my favor by 51 to 49 percent. Am I about to suggest that when the odds are at least 85 to 15 percent in the favor of stocks, you shouldn't take the bet?

A Place for Bonds

Hold on just a minute. I unloaded on the equity gurus because they never seem to acknowledge *any* place for bonds. But if you remember my discussion of gambler's ruin in Chapter 8, you'll recognize the risk in shoving all of your money onto the table for one big bet, even if the odds are in your favor. You could still lose a sizable amount of money. Remember when the stock market fell by more than 40 percent from 1972 to 1975? Remember October 1987? I'm not sure many investors do—but they should. That's one big reason to include bonds in almost any investment portfolio, no matter what your long-term objective.

Another reason to diversify away from 100 percent stocks is paradoxically, the near-universal belief in stocks as the panacea. When investors are so completely convinced that equities are the long-term solution for living on easy street, you just know something must be wrong. There's at least the possibility that we are entering one of the 15 percent periods favoring bond performance, because, as I pointed out throughout Part II of this book, the economy is geared for slow growth. As the highly respected Peter Bernstein, an economist and fund adviser to endowments, writes, "Today's memory banks are stuffed with memories of perpetual upward motion, but believe it or not, life was not ever thus." He points back to periods as recently as six years ago when the doomsayers held sway and "it was good news, not bad news, that was the surprise." And as a final word of caution, he presents a chart of ten-year total returns for stocks, bonds, and short-term paper (Figure 16-2). These are cumulative, not annual, returns, and they begin with the ten-year period ending in 1936 and conclude with the ten-year period from 1986 to 1995. It shows that for most of the stretch, stocks were clearly the winners, but in the early 1970s and for much of that decade, bonds and even short-term cash were superior ten-year performers. In addition, since the mid 1980s, bonds have given stocks a run for their money again.

FIGURE 16-2.
TEN-YEAR TOTAL RETURNS ON STOCKS, BONDS, AND CASH, 1926–36 TO 1986–95

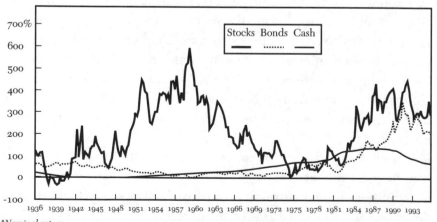

*Nominal returns

Source: Peter L. Bernstein, Inc., January 15, 1996.

These statistics merely remind us of the *possibility* that bonds can do better than stocks during certain longer-term periods of time. It remains to speculate *when* those periods are most likely to occur. Presumably they have something to do with economic growth, profits, and inflation, since those are the three variables that influence the prices of both assets most significantly. If that is the case, the most obvious period of underperformance for stocks—the early 1970s—is a good place to start searching for clues. A steep recession in 1974, anemic corporate profits for the five prior years, and accelerating inflation were the triple whammy that set equities back on their heels. We have *none* of the same conditions today.

"What's your problem then, Mr. Bond?" the equity gurus might ask. Well, it's not a big problem; I'll concede the *probability* of stocks outperforming bonds over the next three to four years. Here's my biggest hang-up, though. Remember my frequent references to the likelihood of 4 to 5 percent *nominal* GDP growth over the next several years? If that becomes a reality, what stock investors have to realize is that GDP is really just another way of describing total national sales. Four to 5 percent nominal increases in GDP mean that U.S. sales or revenues are growing at the same pace—they're the same thing. Think about that for a moment. If sales growth for the S&P 500 were to mimic that of the country as a whole (and it more than likely will), the foundation for profit growth in an economy growing 4 to 5 percent annually would be shaky indeed. For the past few years, earnings have been skyrocketing due to efficiency gains from corporate downsizing and investments in technology. At some point soon, the rate of layoffs will diminish, and the ability of companies to replace people with machines will slow down. I think we're almost there. When that happens, profit growth will be much more closely linked to sales growth and will likely slow to levels of 5 to 6 percent per year.

Right now, few observers can conceive of this reality. Turn on the daily business news and listen to CEO after CEO explain how *his* company is going to increase sales or profits by 20 percent–plus annually. No chance! Maybe a few of them will, but all corporations together will grow only as fast as nominal GDP. Equity investors who envision double-digit gains into the next century for the majority of stocks are dreaming of sugar plums. There is no basis in reality for such visions.

If profit growth is limited by nominal GDP expansion, you have the ingredients of a period during which bonds will outperform stocks—if only slightly and if only by 1 or 2 percent annually. If that's the case, not only should you have *some* bonds in your portfolio, you should think about making them a significant percentage of your holdings. Each person is different, but a 25 to 50 percent concentration in bonds would certainly be prudent in a Butler Creek environment, with some of that devoted to foreign issues and some of it, depending on your tax situation, allocated to municipals.

THE SAVVY INVESTOR:
Municipal Bonds

Municipal bonds appeal to investors because the interest from almost all of them is free from federal taxes. If the issuer happens to be a state or community where you live, you'll pay nothing to the tax man on the local level, either. Because they're tax-free, investors in high income tax brackets are willing to accept a lower rate of interest on municipals than that offered by U.S. Treasury notes and bonds. There is no perfect rule of thumb, but generally, a high-quality municipal bond will yield four fifths, or 80 percent, of its U.S. Treasury equivalent on an equal-maturity basis. Very short munis (one to three years) will yield about 70 percent of Treasuries.

Because of their lower yields, you need to be close to the 30 percent marginal federal tax rate to make the tax-free nature of munis a significant advantage for you. As always, check with your individual tax consultant to verify whether they're appropriate for your own portfolio.

The best advice, though, is not to listen to any guru—even me—as we tout our own particular areas of expertise for the next millennium. Instead, be prepared for the unexpected and *diversify* your portfolio to reflect that which is hard to conceive. And use a three- to five-year secular outlook to influence your conception of the most probable outlook. In doing so, you may not come any closer to defining "Whooo" or what you are, but you'll have opened a clearer path toward long-term investment profits.

SEVENTEEN
Mr. Nietzsche, Meet Mr. Darwin

The Investment Choices You Face

Darwinian man, though well behaved, is really but a monkey shaved.

—W. S. Gilbert

I forget the first time I sat down to the sight of bathroom graffiti. I was probably around seven or eight years old, because that's the age when mothers stop taking their little boys into ladies' room stalls. The women's stalls, at least back then, had nothing but three blank walls to contemplate while sitting on the throne. Entering the brave new world of men's johns, however, I recall quickly encountering a seminal, almost Shakespearean quotation that I could hardly understand, let alone correctly pronounce: "God is dead—Nietzsche. Nietzsche is dead—God." Who was this "Nitch" guy, I thought, and why did he think God was dead? Did God kill *him* because of what he thought? Little did I know that this was my first glimpse into the bottomless chasm of "free will."

Friedrich Nietzsche and his "Superman," you'll remember from your college philosophy course, felt that God was dead because of man's ability to exert his free will. Man could decide his *own* fate. The possibilities and choices were limitless; man, in effect, had become his own god. Well, "Nitch" is dead, of course, and some (perhaps even God) would say none too soon, but the debate about free will rages on. Now, however, it's not philosopher-kings such as Nietzsche who hold center court but the scientists—specifically the genetic scientists who are writing our modern equivalent of bathroom graffiti. "How much of us is in the genes?" *The New York Times* recently asked, and that query, I submit, is *the* question for the twenty-first century, perhaps even for all time, not only on a metaphysical basis but on a sociological and psychological level as well. If it's all in the genes, free will is dead—in fact, it never existed. On the other hand, if genes don't determine everything, both individuals and societies have a chance to determine their own fate.

Many examples in the modern media illustrate the debate. Charles Murray's book *The Bell Curve,* of course, is perhaps the most talked-about example. While it's most commonly cited as a putdown of black people's intelligence, at its heart is the thesis that IQ is significantly a function of hereditary and genetic makeup. Accepting that reality, even if it is true, leads individuals and societies down paths they don't really want to take. It implies that they can't change things much, that they're helpless in the face of immutable chains of DNA that say, "This is the way it will be."

Then there's the current theory (rumored to be funded by the Hugh Hefner Center for Male Sexual Wellness) that *infidelity* is in our genes. Men roam not because they're inherently bad guys but because their genes drive them to produce more and more babies. They even divorce older wives to marry younger women for the same reason. And women, of course, don't get off scot free either. They choose husbands for predominantly genetic reasons as well. If you thought your bride fell in love with you because of your sense of humor, think again. This genetic stuff can get ugly and depressing faster than you can say "Charles Darwin."

Last but not least on my abbreviated list of what's new in genetics is a book by Robert Wright entitled *The Moral Animal*. Mr. Wright claims that seemingly selfless emotions such as love, sympathy, honesty, and gratitude have genetic foundations. In the final analysis, we are not what we eat, we are how we were *born*. In fact, what we eat is mainly determined at the moment of conception. *"Guten Appetit,"* as the Germans would say.

I don't know what to make of all this, but I think about it a lot. Sometimes I think of these genetic theologians as modern counterparts of Copernicus, offering new revelations to a world that still wants to believe the Earth is the center of the universe. Other times I fall back on my old bathroom pal Nietzsche and root for the human spirit and free will. In the final analysis, I know that if it *is* all in the genes, there is no real reason for any of us to be here. Let God produce his prescripted play on some other stage with a different set of genetic automatons. I'll be checking out. That, some might say, is the only bit of free will any of us have after all.

Back to Port

We've come to the end of our journey down Butler Creek, and what better way to end it than with an inquiry into the meaning of existence. Hopefully I've entertained and informed you at the same time. What I hope you've picked up from a financial perspective is that investing in the future will require a different mind-set than the one you or anyone else has had for the past generation or two. Because limited total returns will be available and the investment environment will be less volatile, the investor of the future must approach the markets from a different angle. You should work to reduce the advisory fees you shell out annually, control the emotional aspect of your investment psyche, and focus on the longer-term outlook.

More specifically, you should:

1   Extend the maturity of your bond investments, especially short-term cash.
2   Purchase some inflation-indexed bonds to hedge inflation.

3   Keep a healthy percentage of mortgages in your bond portfolio.

4   Explore international market alternatives, particularly in emerging nations.

5   Consider bonds as an attractive alternative to stocks.

These are strategies I'm employing at Pacific Investment Management Company to invest $90 billion on behalf of our clients. They're the strategies I'll be using to keep us ahead of the pack for the next three years. And if they work for us, they'll work for you too. They won't make you rich quickly. Those days are fading into the past. But they'll give you that extra 1 percent or 2 percent return that will help you navigate Butler Creek in relative comfort—steering a cabin cruiser, perhaps, as opposed to a dugout canoe.

In addition, the economic background briefing provided in Part I of this book should help you plot your own path toward financial success. If you're more of a risk taker than I, think hard about this new global environment and what it suggests for your current portfolio. If you're more conservative, try to incorporate the basic ideas I've tried to advance. If you're not even an investor, well, maybe I've turned on a lightbulb or two and provided a few evenings of pleasurable reading.

Best of luck to you all. For now though, this book is done. All ashore!

Index

Index